The PENNSYLVANIA TURNPIKE PHANTOM KILLER

The PENNSYLVANIA TURNPIKE PHANTOM KILLER

JOHN WESLEY WABLE

RICHARD GAZARIK

THE History PRESS

Published by The History Press
Charleston, SC
www.historypress.com

First published 2022

Manufactured in the United States

ISBN 9781467151603

Library of Congress Control Number: 2022937937

To Adam, Kellie, Katie and John.

CONTENTS

ACKNOWLEDGEMENTS

I remember hearing old-timers talk in the newsroom of the newspaper where I worked about a high-profile murder trial in the 1950s in Greensburg, Pennsylvania, that attracted national attention and raised the issue of freedom of the press. The veteran reporters recounted the killings committed by John Wesley Wable, who stalked sleeping truck drivers along the Pennsylvania Turnpike and shot them in the head. I thought writing a book about Wable would be easy, but then I discovered that court records and the trial transcript from that era no longer exist in the Westmoreland County archives. The key players in this legal drama—Westmoreland County district attorney Alexander Sculco; his assistant, Joseph Loughran; trial judge Edward Bauer; and the defense team, A.C. Scales, B. Patrick Costello and Richard McCormick—are long dead. I was able to recreate Wable's reign of terror from old newspaper clippings from Pennsylvania, Ohio and New Mexico. I was aided by the recollections of attorney John Scales, whose father was the lead defense attorney for Wable, and retired Westmoreland County judge Charles Loughran, whose late father prosecuted Wable. I continue to enjoy the support of my editor, J. Banks Smither, and my wife, Lucy, who serves as my literary compass and managed to turn my manuscript into something readable. Jessica Kiefer's research and documents aided my story. Dave Cole, an electrical engineer, served as my expert in electricity when discussing the electric chair. Thanks also to my daughter, Katie, and son, Adam, for their encouragement.

1
TERROR ON THE TURNPIKE

Truck driver John Shepard was ready to leave work for the day at his job in West Virginia when a last-minute assignment from his employer, Tower Lines, kept him on the road on Friday afternoon, July 31, 1953, a warm and cloudy day in West Virginia's northern panhandle. Shephard had to deliver a shipment of steel from the Wheeling Steel Co. in Beach Bottom, West Virginia, a village along the Ohio River in Brooke County, to the Mullen Manufacturing Co. in Salem, Ohio, south of Youngstown.

Shepard had delivered his load and was headed home for West Alexander, Pennsylvania, when he started dozing off behind the wheel. He pulled his rig off to an isolated spot along Route 30, near Lisbon, Ohio, to catch a few hours of sleep. "When you can't stay awake, boy, you can't stay awake," said Shepard in an interview with the *Pittsburgh Post-Gazette*.

Driving a truck in the early 1950s meant long days and little sleep for truckers, but Shepard had been an army warrant officer during World War II and was accustomed to hauling supplies and troops over long distances in India, Iran and Germany. He lived with his mother and sister on the family farm in West Alexander, located near the northern panhandle of West Virginia. "He usually comes home about two or three times a week," said his sister, Delia Shepard. "Most of the time though he was out on trucking jobs and slept in the cab of his truck," she told the *Pittsburgh Sun-Telegraph*.

Shepard parked his rig at the crest of a knoll known as Green's Hill in Columbiana County. Sleeping compartments in tractor-trailer trucks were just coming into use in 1953, so most drivers still slept on the front seat of their vehicles to save money on motel rooms. The interiors of truck cabs then were spartan compared to later models. They were cramped, had a small fan instead of air conditioning, no power steering and only an AM radio for entertainment. Shepard kicked off his shoes and lay down on the seat. He dozed for a few minutes and suddenly experienced unbearable pain after a loud noise exploded in his right ear. He initially suspected someone had tossed a firecracker into the cab, and then he thought he had suffered a stroke after he saw a river of blood streaming down the side of his face.

"I remember falling asleep, then I heard somebody ask me if I had five dollars. The next thing I heard was the blast, and I was calling for my mother," he told the *Pittsburgh Press* from his hospital bed.

Blood flowed into Shepard's eyes, making it difficult for him to see clearly. He grabbed some paper towels that he kept in the cab and began wiping away the blood when he realized that he had been shot in the head. He stumbled out of the cab and staggered in front of his truck when he saw a pair of headlights from an approaching vehicle coming toward him. The driver got out of the car, walked up to the wounded Shepard and began mumbling something about a killer stalking sleeping truck drivers at night along the Pennsylvania Turnpike. Shepard was unable to understand what the stranger was telling him because he was on the verge of passing out from the pain.

"I got out of the cab and walked around in front of the truck. I was holding my head, and I remember there was blood running down my fingers. Then I saw this man standing there. I never saw him before. I don't know where he came from," the *Pittsburgh Post-Gazette* reported. "You've got a lot of blood there," said the stranger. "How about taking off your pants and using them to wipe it up." Shepard climbed back into the cab and removed his gray work pants and hung them over the steering wheel. The stranger offered to summon an ambulance but told Shepard he didn't have enough gas in his car to return to the scene, so Shepard handed him a five-dollar bill for gas and waited for help to arrive—but the good Samaritan never returned. "That's about all I remember, except my pants disappeared," Shepard said.

Charles Burgess of Loudon, Ohio, was traveling along Route 30 around 3:30 a.m. when he saw Shepard hanging out of his cab, his face covered with blood. "The fellow was kind of babbling. He didn't know what really happened," Burgess told the *Pittsburgh Press*. Burgess flagged down a car driven by Ford Keck, who was returning home from a fishing trip with his wife and son when he saw Burgess waving furiously alongside the roadway.

After stopping, Keck sped the two miles to Salem City for help while Burgess stayed with Shepard. Lisbon police officer John Holshue arrived, saw Shepherd's bloody face and mistakenly concluded that Shepherd had been the victim of a beating. "It wasn't until we got him to the hospital that we realized he was shot," Holshue said.

A passing truck driver, Roderick Williamson of Canton, Ohio, told police that he saw Shepard's truck just as a blue 1952 Chevrolet sped past him headed west. He didn't recognize the driver but later told police that the car had Pennsylvania license plates. Williamson remembered four digits of the car's plate, which led Ohio state police to trace six hundred plates containing similar numbers.

Surgeons dug a bullet out of Shepard's head at Salem City Hospital. The slug had traveled downward from behind his right ear and become lodged in his jaw, just missing his brain. In addition to his pants, Shepard also was missing his gold Elgin pocket watch, which would be a key piece of evidence in the investigation. Shepard's mother, Agnes, was at her son's bedside after he returned from surgery. "We can just hope for the best," she told the *Wheeling Intelligencer*.

A headline in the July 3, 1953 edition of the *Pittsburgh Press* blared, "The Turnpike Phantom Strikes Again." Shepard didn't realize at the time that he had come face to face with a killer dubbed by newspapers as the "Turnpike Phantom."

Lester Woodward was headed east along the Pennsylvania Turnpike, headed home to Duncannon, Pennsylvania, after delivering four new Pontiacs from Flint, Michigan, to a Pittsburgh car dealership. Woodward was tired and planned to bed down for the night before resuming his 152-mile drive to Perry County in the morning. He parked his tractor trailer truck in a foggy, secluded area near the Irwin Interchange on July 26, 1953, and lay down on the seat of his cab. Early the next morning, the body of thirty-year-old Woodward was found by two men. He had been shot in the head. Woodward, who worked for John Reeser Trucking of Duncannon, got on the turnpike near the Ohio border on Friday at 7:32 p.m., according to a toll ticket found in his truck. His empty wallet was found on the floor of the cab, and police suspected the motive of the murder was robbery, although investigators did not know how much cash, if any, Woodward was carrying.

Jim Veitch, who lived near the pike, and a friend, Glenn Maroney, were approached by a man driving a green Buick who stopped and asked for help. "The driver of that truck is laying in his cab with his head all bloody," the motorist said. Veitch noticed that Woodward's truck had been parked in the same spot in the eastbound lane for about eighteen hours. Curious, Veitch asked W.H. Weston, the owner of a nearby service station, to accompany him to the scene. Veitch saw Woodard's body and noticed his face and hair were covered with dried blood.

"Jim Veitch was building a home near the turnpike. He noticed the truck had been parked on the shoulder for quite a while. He came down to the station and asked me to walk up to see what was wrong with it," Weston told the *Pittsburgh Sun-Telegraph* in an interview. "The driver was slumped across the front seat in a pool of blood. We didn't move him. We went straight back and called state police."

An autopsy revealed the bullet entered Woodward's left temple and traveled downward, just missing his jugular vein. Woodward wasn't the only casualty that night. Investigators said the time of Woodward's death coincided with a fiery six-vehicle accident in the westbound lane one hundred yards away that killed two Cleveland women and injured seven others. State police initially suspected the accident was the result of a chain reaction, but troopers discovered tire tracks leading from the eastbound lane of the murder scene that cut across the medial strip and into the westbound lane. They theorized that whoever shot Woodward may have fled in haste in the other direction in front of the oncoming vehicles, triggering the accident. Four cars and two tractor trailer trucks collided on the fog-shrouded roadway, clogging traffic for miles, according to the *Pittsburgh Sun-Telegraph*.

Trucker Herbert Parr was traveling on the turnpike on July 28 and was surprised to see the tractor trailer truck belonging to his childhood friend Harry Franklin Pitts, thirty-nine, of Bowling Green, Virginia, parked near the Donegal Interchange. He immediately recognized the copper-colored horns on Pitts's truck and wondered why Pitts had stopped. Both drivers had delivered new cars to Pittsburgh, and Parr just thought his friend had overslept.

"I braked my truck down to go over and wake him up," Parr told the *Pittsburgh Press*. Instead, he found his friend's shoeless body hanging out the door. There were two other trucks parked a short distance behind Pitts. Parr flagged down another truck and ordered the driver to travel to the next interchange and notify state police. "On the way, I hollered to the drivers of the other two trucks parked behind his. I was afraid to go back there to those trucks because I might find the same thing there."

Police immediately linked the shooting of Shepard and the murders of Woodward and Pitts, because the gunman used a .32-caliber, German-made Walther pistol in all three incidents. "We think the same person shot all three men," said Captain John Miller of the Ohio Highway Patrol. Columbiana County sheriff Howard Clark told reporters that police were looking for a madman. "He's either a maniac or someone out to get all trucks because a truck driver killed a member of his family," the *Pittsburgh Press* reported.

A German-made Walther pistol like the one used by Wable to kill two truck drivers and wound a third. *From Wikipedia.*

Pennsylvania State Police were already investigating two unsolved murders that occurred along the turnpike in 1951. Then, on August 7, 1953, the state police found the bodies of a husband and wife near the scene where Woodward was murdered. Investigators thought the phantom killer had struck again, but an investigation revealed the couple had died by suicide. Turner and Mary Ruff had shot themselves and left a note, explaining they were penniless, homeless and hungry. "Its [*sic*] the end of the trail for us. We tried, but without a home and no money, it got too tough. Thanks to so many people who really tried, we were able to get this far," read the note, which was published in the *Pittsburgh Press*.

The killing of the two truckers ignited an intensive investigation by the Pennsylvania State Police, which began stopping and questioning hitchhikers. They investigated a red-haired woman who lived along the turnpike and was known to be friendly with truckers. They also investigated a British war bride and her lesbian lover who ran a brothel that catered to truckers, according the *Pittsburgh Post-Gazette*. In Norwalk, Ohio, police received a report of a driver scaring off a man who approached his truck in the darkness. Police learned the man's identity and discovered he was a minister. He passed a lie detector test after explaining his presence on the highway. "I was hunting women," he said. "I must have been crazy," reported the *Pittsburgh Post-Gazette*.

State police questioned two young hitchhikers who were found sleeping at the Jefferson Memorial in Washington, D.C., because they had a .32-caliber pistol in their possession. Detroit police stopped a man for a routine traffic stop and discovered a .32-caliber handgun in his car; they notified the state police in Pennsylvania. The three individuals were cleared as suspects.

Investigators also began looking for a link between the turnpike killings and the October 1951 slaying of Andrew Pfister, which was the first murder in the history of the turnpike. The thirty-seven-year-old Pittsburgh man and father of four pulled up to the tollbooth at the Monroeville Interchange near

Pittsburgh with a young, dirty and disheveled-looking passenger sitting next to him. Pfister seemed tense. The toll taker John Sands sensed by the look on Pfister's face that Pfister was in danger. "I couldn't see the killer's face so good, as we usually pay more attention to the driver. I did see the passenger's hand going into his hip pocket," Sands told the *Pittsburgh Sun-Telegraph*. "He seemed to shrink away to my side of the car. Suddenly, I saw the gun and heard the shots. At the last minute, the other man shoved a gun into the driver's side. He had a wild look….I knew something was going to happen right then."

Pfister was shot four times before his body tumbled out of the driver's side and onto the pavement. The gunman jumped out of the car and fired two more shots at Sands before jumping over a fence and fleeing into the nearby woods. "It sounded like kids with cap pistols. The windows of the car were down. Then he pointed a gun at me. There was a wild look in his eyes. I had been shot at before in the army, and I jumped away and started to pull the door shut on the tollhouse when he fired at me. I shouted, 'Look out!' and dropped to the floor."

A short time after Pfister was killed, a cab driver was hijacked at gunpoint in nearby Swissvale and forced to drive seven miles to downtown Pittsburgh. Over one hundred police officers cordoned off the Golden Triangle, where the Allegheny and Monongahela Rivers form the Ohio River, searching for a suspect who matched the description of Pfister's killer. Police launched a massive manhunt using volunteers and an airplane from the Civil Air Patrol that flew at treetop level over the woods searching for the suspect. Police stopped more than one hundred cars, buses and trucks and scoured hotels and boardinghouses for the suspect. But despite an intensive search, the gunman evaded capture.

While police searched for the killer, a dirty, disheveled man approached cabbie Morris Wasserman for a ride. "It was because he was so dirty that I didn't want him in the cab, but he opened the door and got in beside me. Right away, he brought out a gun," said Wasserman. The gunman ordered him to drive into downtown Pittsburgh. After the man got inside, the taxi company dispatcher radioed Wasserman to pick up a fare, but Wasserman responded using a distress signal to alert the dispatcher that he was in trouble. He added the number 7 to his cab number, 203, as a plea for help, but the gunman got out of the vehicle and looked at the cab's number. "He asked me why I said seven in my call, but I told him that just meant I wouldn't be calling in again until seven o'clock," Wasserman told the *Pittsburgh Press*. "It was the only thing I could think of, and it didn't sound so good. I really thought my number was up. But for some reason, the guy told me to keep driving until I got downtown."

He said the gunman demanded the eight dollars Wasserman had on him, but the cabbie talked him out of it. "Why stick me up for peanuts when you can get some real dough?" The man said he was going to rob the ticket agent at the Greyhound bus station. "We can pull it together," said the man. As the suspect got out of the car, Wasserman floored it and fled in his cab. The suspected killer was last seen in an alley behind a movie theater.

John Cehovsky became a suspect in Pfister's murder after he was involved in a seven-hour gun battle with police in the South Hills of Pittsburgh in January 1952. Although he was never linked to the killing, Cehovsky was convicted for shooting at police officers and sentenced to twenty to forty years in prison. He had previously served a decade in an Oregon prison for kidnapping. Allegheny County detective Kenneth Baird said the investigation into Pfister's slaying was hampered by a lack of a clear description of the suspect. "All we know [is that] he was a white man. We don't have a description of him," Baird told the *Sun-Telegraph*.

A rumor surfaced after Pitts was murdered that the state police had arrested a suspect, but Lieutenant Eugene Fontaine of the Greensburg station quicky squelched the report. "It's not true we have a suspect," Fontaine told the *Pittsburgh Press*. "We have questioned a lot of people as witnesses but none as suspects."

Pennsylvania investigators took every lead seriously, since the phantom had shot three drivers between July 26 and July 31, and they feared he would soon strike again. Meanwhile, troopers received alerts about possible suspects from other jurisdictions that they had to investigate. New York City detectives asked the Pennsylvania State Police to compare slugs from a pistol that was used to kill a bar owner to the bullets used in the Woodward and Pitts slayings, but three suspects were later arrested in that case. Detectives thought they had the killer after a man "confessed" to a priest in Philadelphia that he was the Turnpike Phantom. William Woollam, thirty-four, went to the Church of the Visitation and told the Reverend John Larkin he was responsible for the turnpike murders. After talking to police, they discounted Woollam's story, characterizing him as a "dangerous mental case," and committed him to a mental hospital, according to the *Philadelphia Inquirer.*

William J. Town confessed to killing a priest, the Reverend Robert Hodges, in Indiana, but Town denied he was the Turnpike Phantom, according to the *New York Times*. Leo Baumgardner was drinking in a Fayette County bar, boasting that he had shot Andrew Pfister, but Baumgardner denied he was the killer, despite five hours of interrogation. He said he had served time on a North Carolina chain gang and was in Uniontown on the day Pfister was killed, according to the *Pittsburgh Press.*

A man resembling Bumgardner was suspected of carjacking cab driver Nick Sivily and forcing him to drive to a secluded spot in Pittsburgh's Schenley Park. The suspect stole Sivily's money and locked him in the trunk of his cab. Baumgardner was cleared of the Pfiester killing after passing a polygraph test. A gun-waving man pointed a weapon at a passing truck in York, Pennsylvania. Another man with a gun tried to stop a truck in Clairton, near Pittsburgh, but investigations indicated none involved were linked to the turnpike murders.

A U.S. marine on a weekend pass was beaten to death with a hammer in 1951 off the Breezewood Interchange near Bedford. Sergeant Robert Wright was returning to Washington, D.C., after visiting a girlfriend in Youngstown, Ohio. His car was found abandoned forty miles away from the murder scene. Barbara Lutes said Wright arrived at her home after driving all night from Alexandria, Virginia. They spent the day together before he left. Wright suffered a fractured skull and died in a local hospital. State police said the hammer used appeared to be the type truckers used to change tires. "I can't believe it. I can't believe it," she told the *Bedford Gazette.*

Two men were questioned in Pittsburgh after police found them in possession of a .32-caliber pistol, but ballistics tests later cleared them of any involvement in the turnpike killings. A newlywed couple from Boston, Massachusetts, were arrested near Pittsburgh for financing their cross-country honeymoon with a string of armed robberies using a .32-caliber gun. A gun-toting man threatened a truck driver in York County, Pennsylvania, and another driver reported that a motorist passed his vehicle on the turnpike while waving a pistol at him.

Pittsburgh police arrested William Kerr, who admitted to killing a housewife in 1950 and a bakery worker in 1953, and they were eager to question him about the turnpike killings but ruled him out after questioning, the *Pittsburgh Press* reported. Investigators thought they had captured the killer in August 1953, after Ohio police arrested an AWOL soldier for killing an Ohio state official near Zanesville. Harold St. John, twenty-five, of Dorchester, Massachusetts, confessed to shooting Joseph W. Harding, fifty-three, during an attempted robbery after Harding gave the hitchhiking St. John a lift. Police cleared St. John of the Pennsylvania Turnpike murders after they learned he was in the stockade when the murders had occurred in July.

A truck driver told police he was followed from Delaware to Aberdeen, Maryland, by a man driving a car and wearing a hooded jacket. Police located the driver, who turned out to be a college football player wearing a team parka. He pulled the hood over his head because he was cold while driving with the windows open in the cool night air.

The Pennsylvania State Police tried to trap the killer by parking trucks occupied by troopers along deserted areas of the turnpike, but the killer failed to take the bait. Truck drivers were in a panic and began traveling in convoys and carrying weapons to protect themselves. Troopers ordered truckers to "keep it rolling" and to stop only at well-lighted rest areas or gas stations. Frank Restivo told a reporter for the *Pittsburgh Press* that exhaustion wasn't a luxury drivers could afford. "What are you going to do when you get so tired you weave all over the road? You can't keep going for a gas station." Restivo armed himself with a three-foot-long crowbar in his cab. "If I'm going to stop, I'm going to stop, and if anybody tries to shoot me, I'm going to put up a fight. I'll tell you one thing, if this keeps up, we're going to start carrying guns, law or no law."

E.C. Mason was on his way to Toledo, Ohio, and didn't plan to make any more stops until he reached home. "Anybody who'd knock off two drivers is crazy enough to try for three. Me, I'm highballin' off this turnpike after I leave this stop." Herbert Coates was on his way to Pittsburgh from Philadelphia. "Either there's an idiot loose on the turnpike or someone's gunning for somebody. I figure maybe he got the wrong man the first time, then read about it in the paper and went right back to get the right one on the second try."

A Pennsylvania state trooper wakes a sleeping truck driver along the turnpike and warns him to keep moving following the murders of two drivers. *Courtesy of the* Sun-Telegraph.

Turnpikes and major highways have always been dangerous places—and not just because of accidents. They also became fertile hunting grounds for serial killers, since nearly forty-three thousand miles of roads were built in the United States in the 1950s. This proliferation of killings forced the FBI to create the Highway Serial Killer Initiative to solve some of the hundreds of unsolved homicide cases that occurred along the nation's highways.

Meanwhile, Pennsylvania and Ohio state troopers continued pursuing leads they hoped would lead them to the killer. Police in both states had the killer in their clutches at some point but didn't realize it at the time and let him go. A twenty-four-year-old drifter, John Wesley Wable, who lived in the backwoods village of Ohiopyle in southwestern Pennsylvania, had been arrested in Uniontown, Pennsylvania, for stealing a car. He admitted to a cellmate that he was the Turnpike Phantom Killer but was released because no one believed his story. When officials realized he was the prime suspect, it was too late. Wable was on the run.

2
IF IT BLEEDS, IT LEADS

Crime stories have long been a staple of newspapers, and reporters were drawn to the turnpike killings like sharks are attracted to blood in the water. Editors dubbed the suspect the "Phantom Turnpike Killer," and the murders dominated the news coverage for the rest of the year as the investigations continued.

The Puritans of early Massachusetts, those straitlaced, somber-looking clerics, stood on the gallows next to an individual who waited to enter eternity at the end of a rope as the black-robed minister delivered an "execution sermon," recounting the details of the crime and the condemned's miserable life, according to *Mortal Remains: Death in Early America*. Ministers were "gray old Gospellers, sour as midwinter," according to a description of Puritan clergy in *Two Centuries of Costume in America*.

The sermons were, in a sense, true crime narratives that contained details of the crime and perhaps the prisoner's confession accompanied by a fire and brimstone oration based on passages from the Bible, according to "In Defense of the Gallows: Justification of Capital Punishment in New England Execution Sermons, 1674–1825" in *American Quarterly*. The sermons had all the elements that comprise true crime books today—interesting characters, strong storytelling and details of the crime that appealed to people's fascination with evil. The sermons made ministers like Increase and Cotton Mather, Samuel Danforth and Benjamin Coleman the first true crime authors. Although the sermons were aimed at sin and salvation, some ministers, such as Cotton Mather, made them appeal to a broader audience by adding "a dollop or two of sensationalism."

The sermons were not meant to titillate observers but to instill in them the fear of God. Puritan ministers viewed the sermons as an opportunity to save the souls of the thousands who attended the hangings and served to justify the righteousness of the execution. The sermons had the opposite effect. They appealed to the crowd because they contained the condemned individual's confession, lurid details of the crime and the state of the prisoner's mind before they died. To appeal to a broader audience, the sermons were published by the ministers and sold at a low cost to a public who craved the details of the execution.

In 1635 in England, John Reynolds published *The Triumphe of God's Revenge Against Execrable Sinn of Murther*, a compilation of tales about executions. "They certainly pull you in. Human nature doesn't change. There is morbid fascination," according to "Guide to the Gallows" in *The Harvard Gazette*. The execution sermons are part of a collection, "Dying Speeches and Bloody Murders," at the Harvard Law School Library. The first known execution sermon was delivered in 1674 by Samuel Danforth and was titled "The Cry of Sodom Inquired Into." It was delivered at the execution of a man who was hanged for bestiality. "You pity his youth and tender years, [but] I pray, pity the holy law of God, which is shamefully violated…pity the land, which is fearfully polluted and defiled."

To the Puritans, executions were a way of avenging God for the sins of man. Increase Mather in Massachusetts delivered a warning at the execution of a convicted murder in 1686, saying that the state had a legal and moral obligation to kill those who "violated the laws of God," according to the book *Hanging Between Heaven and Earth, Execution Preaching and Theology in Early New England*. "One murderer unpunished may bring guilt and a curse upon the whole land, that all the inhabitants of the land shall suffer for it," Mather warned. The Puritans wanted the sermons to impress upon the witnesses the dangers of sin and to serve as a deterrence to future crimes.

The prisoner was expected to participate in this theater of death by confessing, seeking repentance and asking for God's forgiveness. The sermons, containing the last mutterings of the executed and details of the crime, were printed and sold to a populace eager to read about how the condemned behaved before dying. A condemned person's last words were likely written by a minister or a public official who spent time with the prisoner before his death.

Ministers later added details of the crime and execution, which were read aloud to the crowd. The sermons included the word-for-word confession and verbatim conversations between the condemned and his jailers, because the Puritans realized they could avert future sin if they sensationalized the details to make an impression on individuals. In one sermon, the confession of a man who was about to hang for murdering his family described in detail each step he took and the order in which the victims were murdered. In another case, a man who was about to die for rape and murder detailed how he hid in the woods and ambushed a young woman.

"They certainly pulled you in," said Mary Person, an archivist at the Harvard Law School Library, which compiled a collection of execution sermons, "Dying Speeches and Bloody Murders."

In Pennsylvania, chapbooks, known as "gallows literature," were inexpensive and small—four by eight inches—and ran between eight and twelve pages in length. The pages were published in boldface type and often contained woodcuts of the gallows and coffins, with figures hanging at the end of ropes, according to "Chapbook Gallows Literature in Nineteenth-Century Pennsylvania" published in *Pennsylvania Folklife*. John H. Craig's execution was memorialized in an 1818 chapbook, which heralded, "The confession of John H. Craig and executed on Saturday, the sixth of June 1818, for the murder of Edward Hunter, Esq., as stated by him after trial."

True crime stories took hold during the Elizabethan era, according to Laura Browder's article "True Crime," which appeared in 2010 in the *Cambridge Companion to American Crime Fiction*. *In Cold Blood* by Truman Capote was the first modern crime book and detailed the 1959 murders of the four members of the Clutter family in Holcomb, Kansas. Capote merged journalism and creative writing in a nonfiction book that read like a novel. *In Cold Blood* was followed by Vincent Bugliosi's *Helter Skelter*, an account of the Manson family murders; Joe McGinnis's tale of Green Beret captain Jeffrey MacDonald's slaying of his wife and two children; Jack Olsen's *Salt of the Earth: One Family's Journey Through the Violent American Landscape*; and Ann Rule's book on serial killer Ted Bundy, *The Stranger Beside Me*.

True crime books were a far cry from early newspaper accounts of murders, trials and executions. A reporter for the *Uniontown Morning Herald* in Pennsylvania who witnessed the execution of John Kozial in the electric chair in 1933 was less than literary when he wrote, "In a flash, it was over—John William Kozial had gone to a higher court to receive a sentence that is to last through eternity."

George Edward Stevenson killed a constable in Pennsylvania, fled to West Virginia and was cornered by a posse, shot and left paralyzed. A reporter for the *Pittsburgh Press* wrote in 1925 that "Stevenson was paralyzed from the waist down, and four guards had to carry him on a stretcher and lifted him onto the electric chair, where he was soon paralyzed from the head down."

Crime stories first surfaced in the 1830s, when Benjamin Day of the *New York Sun* titillated readers with tales of murder and mayhem. "If it bleeds, it leads" became the editorial philosophy of newspapers. Edmund Pearson, in 1924, wrote *Studies in Murder*, which is considered a classic in the true crime genre. Pearson was a Harvard-educated librarian who defined "true crime" with his writings about murder and mayhem.

Even the Bible is considered a true crime book, with Old Testament tales of murder and violence starting in Genesis with the story of Cain and Abel, the sons of Adam and Eve. Cain slays his brother and is punished by being forced to wander the rest of his life. Amnon, a son of King David, is slain for raping his half sister. Even God doesn't escape murder accusations. He destroyed the cities of Sodom and Gomorrah and turned Lot's wife into a pillar of salt. He also killed the firstborn sons of Egypt and destroyed the entire Egyptian army in the Red Sea.

Ever since Jack the Ripper terrorized London, readers have been drawn to the gory details of murder, which spawned a tabloid culture that focuses on sensational murders and celebrity gossip. The best example of this form of journalistic culture was the 1983 *New York Post* headline "Headless Man Slain in Topless Bar."

3

DREAM HIGHWAY

To build the initial 160-mile stretch of the Pennsylvania Turnpike, workers used 2.2 million barrels of cement, eight hundred thousand tons of sand, fifty tons of steel and $30 million worth of equipment. The project employed fifteen thousand men and cost the state $61 million to construct what was billed as the "dream highway" when it opened in 1940, according to the *Bulletin Index*, a Pittsburgh-based magazine. "At midnight, two black cats ambled across the gleaming cement. A minute later, a ticket seller dropped his arm in the gesture of an automobile race-starter, and the traffic was underway," reported the *Harrisburg Telegraph*.

Toll taker Morris Neiberg handed Carl Boe of McKeesport in Allegheny County a ticket, and Boe became the first motorist to enter the turnpike at the Irwin Interchange. No sooner was Boe underway when he was flagged down by two men, Frank Lorey, twenty-three, and Dick Gangle, twenty-one, who became the first people to hitch a ride on the turnpike. The day after the road's dedication, more than ten thousand vehicles jammed the interchanges, tying up traffic for miles. Five-mile-long traffic jams prevented motorists from getting off or on the turnpike, the *Pittsburgh Post-Gazette* reported.

There was no speed limit on the turnpike, which ran from Irwin in Westmoreland County in the west to Carlisle in Cumberland County in the east, during the highway's early years of operation. Shortly after the road opened, A.E. Weaver of Akron, Ohio, was traveling eighty miles an hour in his eleven-ton truck when he noticed he was being followed by a Pennsylvania

A photograph of early construction of the Pennsylvania Turnpike. *From the National Archives.*

state trooper. Weaver was nervous, so he pulled off the road to see if the trooper would pass him, but the patrol car followed Weaver and came to a halt behind his tractor trailer. The trooper got out of his vehicle and approached Weaver. "How'd you like the road?" the trooper asked. "It's very nice," Weaver replied. "I guess I get a ticket." "No, we aren't interested in the speed limit….We won't bother you," according to an article in the Pennsylvania Center for the Book at Penn State University.

Building the Pennsylvania Turnpike was viewed by government officials as a solution to a problem that plagued travelers who were trying to get from one end of the state to the other. The massive Appalachian Mountains served as a barrier to fast and direct travel, so in 1934, Victor Lecog of the Pennsylvania Planning Commission and William Sutherland of the Pennsylvania Motor Truck Association proposed the idea of building a toll road across the state to connect the state's two major cities, Pittsburgh and Philadelphia. They envisioned a highway without any red lights that would allow vehicles to zip across Pennsylvania by utilizing tunnels through the mountains.

The turnpike's path followed the route first used by William Vanderbilt, the owner of the New York Central and Hudson River Railroad, which was in competition for business with the Pennsylvania Railroad. Vanderbilt embarked on a project to build the South Pennsylvania Railroad line parallel to the route used by the Pennsylvania Railroad, but the project was abandoned in 1885 in what became known as "Vanderbilt's Folly."

President Franklin D. Roosevelt was intrigued by the project and thought highway construction was a way to reduce unemployment during the Great Depression, but Pennsylvania was nearly broke and unable to finance the work, so Roosevelt tapped into the New Deal to pay for it. The Reconstruction Finance Corporation and the Public Works Administration provided the money to build the turnpike. The Public Works Administration was created in 1933 and was used to finance the building of roads, bridges and dams. The Reconstruction Finance Corporation was created under President Herbert Hoover, but its funding and powers to finance projects were expanded under Roosevelt. The roadway was such a financial success that by the early 1950s, 12 million vehicles had used the superhighway, generating $20 million in revenue at a penny a mile, according to the *New York Times*

The *New York Times* referred to the turnpike as an "American epic in concrete flowing through the forests and fields of Pennsylvania with the antic ease of a carpet unrolling in an animated cartoon movie." The opening of the turnpike shortened the trip between Pittsburgh and Philadelphia by hours and many miles. The twelve-foot-wide lanes were separated by ten-foot-wide medial strips consisting of grass and trees. Gas stations and restaurants were positioned twelve miles apart so drivers could eat and refuel their vehicles without having to get off and on the turnpike, according to a 1953 edition of *Landscape Architecture* magazine. The pavement was smooth, the grades slight and the curves gentle, but the rising number of accidents, deaths and injuries caused by speeding vehicles prompted Governor Arthur James to warn that "the Pennsylvania dream highway must not be allowed to become a nightmare of fatal accidents."

Top: The turnpike's straight lanes cut the time and distance between the eastern and western end of the state. The lanes were built parallel to the rail lines that were once used by the Pennsylvania Railroad. *From the National Archives.*

Bottom: A Pennsylvania Turnpike sign. *From Wikipedia.*

Since the turnpike's opening in 1940, five hundred motorists had been killed by 1953. By 1951, the turnpike's accident rate was three times worse than that of highways in other states, according to the *Journal of Criminal Law, Criminology and Police Science*. Legislators demanded the state hire more troopers to patrol the turnpike or to allow the Turnpike Commission to create its own police force. A highway safety expert said the lack of a speed limit was tantamount to murder or suicide. A seventy-mile-per-hour speed limit was enacted, but lawmakers urged Governor John Fine to reduce speeds to sixty miles per hour and erect barriers between opposing lanes to prevent out-of-control vehicles from crossing into the east- or westbound lanes and crashing into one another.

Bus crashes were the causes of several fatal accidents, according to the Pennsylvania Public Utility Commission. Five Greyhound bus passengers were killed and twenty-five injured in 1953 due to speeding. The rural town of Bedford in Bedford County, which runs near the turnpike midway between Pittsburgh and Harrisburg, knew firsthand the impact of speeding. At first, Bedford had one lot in which to store the wrecks pulled from the turnpike, but by 1951, it had six lots containing over seven hundred crumpled hulks.

The early turnpike had no medial barriers to prevent cars from swerving into opposite lanes. *From the National Archives.*

State senator John Dent of Westmoreland County said the "dream highway" was turning into the "nightmare highway" because of the death toll and complained to the *Pittsburgh Press* that the "the turnpike commissioners draw their salaries and are doing nothing. The turnpike is getting a bad reputation throughout the nation, and the people are afraid of it." State senator Joe Barr of Pittsburgh wanted more state troopers hired to patrol the roadway. "Two brutal murders on the turnpike at night within a week show clearly that more police protection is needed on the toll road."

While lawmakers and traffic experts debated the cause of such a high accident rate, the number of fatalities continued to increase. The Turnpike Commission reported that there were 138 accidents resulting in five deaths in 1940, the year the roadway opened. Those numbers rose to 1,832 accidents and eighty-three fatalities by 1952, but the commission refused to blame the speed limit for the increase. There were three deaths within five days on the turnpike in April 1953 and another four near the Irwin Interchange that same month. Five were killed and thirty-one injured in a bus crash in June. Two children and a soldier died in August, followed by the death of three more children in September along the turnpike in Somerset. "The whir of the tires on the speeding passenger cars is like the rustling wings of the Angel of Death," editorialized the *Pittsburgh Sun-Telegraph* in a call for reducing the speed limit. Governor James suggested a fifty-mile-per-hour speed limit, but his recommendation was ignored, even though vehicles were being clocked going as fast as eighty-five miles an hour, with little or no effort from the state police to enforce a speed limit, according to three Pittsburgh newspapers.

Traveling on the turnpike was a long, lonely and dangerous trek for truck drivers, who communicated by flashing their headlights or using hand signals to alert fellow drivers of state police lurking nearby, traffic tie-ups or dangers along the roadway. Citizens band radios, cellphones and global positioning systems hadn't been invented yet, and neither had call boxes that could be used by motorists to call for help in an emergency.

Meanwhile, the manhunt for the Phantom Killer led police across the country from the backwoods of Pennsylvania to Ohio and New Mexico before ending in a courtroom in Greensburg, Pennsylvania, with the trial of a tall, skinny drifter from the backwoods of southwestern Pennsylvania.

4

THE POCKET WATCH

Pennsylvania state trooper Jerome McCavitt arrived at the West Alexander home of John Shepard shortly after he was shot to question his family about the missing yellow gold Elgin pocket watch that Shepard was carrying when he was shot while sleeping in his truck. West Alexander is a quaint village where some of its structures have stood since the eighteenth century. The community was referred to as the "Gretna Green" of Pennsylvania, a popular place for runaway couples from Ohio and West Virginia to marry since Pennsylvania, at the time, did not require a marriage license, according to the *Pittsburgh Press*. The nickname referred to the Scottish village of Gretna Green that was popular with underage couples (under twenty-one years old) in England and Wales who wanted to get married but lacked parental consent. Any resident of Gretna Green could officiate a marriage as long as two witnesses were present for the ceremony.

James Gashel, Shepard's brother-in-law, owned an identical pocket watch because he and Shepard had purchased the timepieces at the same time for $42.50 each from Posin's Jewelry Co. in the city of Wheeling, West Virginia. Gashel's wife, Jean, had taken Shepard's fifteen-jewel watch to a jeweler in Washington, Pennsylvania, to be repaired, and the jeweler etched the serial number J-106082 on the case. McCavitt took Gashel's watch, photographed it and distributed a flyer with the picture to pawnshops in Pennsylvania, Ohio and West Virginia in the hopes that the killer may have pawned the watch for cash.

An Elgin watch like the timepiece stolen from John Shepard. *From the Elgin Watch Co.*

Samuel Scragg was working at the David Loan Co. in Cleveland when he received a copy of the flyer. Scragg immediately checked his inventory of watches and found the model with the same serial number. Scragg told Cleveland homicide detectives George Gackowski and Louis Jalovec that a man had pawned the watch for ten dollars on August 4, five days after Shepard was shot, but never returned to redeem it. Scragg recalled, however, that the man wore a company work shirt with the name "Parker Appliance Co." stenciled above the breast pocket. The customer signed the pawn ticket "John Maple." Parker Appliance manufactured pneumatic brake systems for large trucks and buses before becoming Parker Hannifin Manufacturing Co. in 1957.

The detectives went to Parker Appliance and learned the firm did not have an employee named Maple on its payroll, but it had employed a John Wesley Wable, who had quit a week earlier. Then they caught another break. John Jandura, the stepfather of Wable's girlfriend, Leora Crissey, in Bedford Heights, outside Cleveland, turned over to police a .32-caliber Walther pistol that Wable had hidden in Jandura's home. Crissey told John Jandura that Wable had hidden the weapon, bullets and a shoulder holster in a china closet because she was nervous about having the gun in the house around her three-year-old daughter. The gun was turned over to the Pennsylvania State Police for testing against the bullets that were used to kill Lester Woodward and Harry Pitts and wound Shepard. They were a match. "Well, that does it. Wable is our man," said Pennsylvania State Police major Andrew Hudock to the *Pittsburgh Press.*

Cleveland police continued their investigation without knowing that John Wesley Wable was in the Fayette County Jail in Uniontown, Pennsylvania, for failing to return a rental car that he had used to drive back and forth between Pennsylvania and Ohio for three weeks, putting five thousand miles on the odometer. On one of his trips back home to Ohiopyle in Fayette County, Wable was driving the car when Francis Palumbo, the manager of the rental car agency, saw the vehicle that Wable had rented parked at a restaurant on Route 40, outside of Uniontown. Palumbo was going in the opposite direction, so he turned his car around and headed back toward the restaurant. As Palumbo arrived at the parking lot, Wable recognized him and took off. Palumbo gave chase. Wable led Palumbo on a reckless ride through the lot of a drive-in theater, accelerating the car and kicking up a cloud of dust and rocks. Palumbo wanted to avoid damaging his car, so he got out of the vehicle and chased Wable on foot, but Wable nearly ran him over, grazing him as he sped past.

Wable drove to Cleveland after the incident and was arrested in August after getting into a fight with two soldiers who accused him of stealing their wallets. He was returned to Pennsylvania, where he faced arraignment on a federal charge of interstate flight to avoid prosecution. However, the FBI asked that the hearing be delayed, so Wable was taken to Uniontown and housed in the Fayette County Jail to await his court appearance. Wable was in the Fayette County Jail from mid-August to mid-October 1953. His cellmate, Charlie Welch, was an acquaintance who was serving a sentence for a parole violation.

One day, Wable casually asked Welch what would happen to the killer of the truck drivers if the man ever was caught. Welch said he didn't know and dismissed the conversation as jailhouse chatter until Wable made a startling admission that would come back to haunt him. "What do you think a guy would get for something like that if he got caught?" asked Wable. "I don't know," replied Welch. "Well, I did it," said Wable. The state police hadn't released the name of the suspect in the turnpike killings, but Joe Bianco, a reporter for the *Patriot News* in Harrisburg, Pennsylvania, had been reporting on the killings and learned about Wable's admission. Bianco identified Wable by name and reported that Wable had given Welch Shepard's pants. (Bianco's scoop earned him a nomination for a Pulitzer Prize for local reporting and an eventual share of the reward money for Wable's capture.) By the time the story was published, Wable had been released because his father had paid the car company $1,100 as restitution. Wable promised his father to pay him back for the car, but he never made good on his promise, as he quit his job in Cleveland. "That's like him to do that," his mother told a reporter for the *Pittsburgh Press*.

5

OHIOPYLE

John Wesley Wable began life in the backwoods of Ohiopyle, deep in the mountains and forests of Fayette County. Ohiopyle is located along the Youghiogheny River, which flows through the tiny hamlet that is surrounded by twenty thousand acres of forest filled with bald cypress, large-leaf magnolia, oak and hemlock trees. The whitewater lapping over large boulders embedded in the river makes sections of the Youghiogheny River treacherous to rafters and canoeists who challenge the river every year. Dimple Rock is a large, triangular-shaped sandstone boulder that has been the scene of nearly two dozen deaths over the years. Capsized rafters are sucked beneath the rock and drowned.

Ohiopyle is located sixty miles south of Pittsburgh and is home to Ohiopyle State Park, a popular tourist destination for rafting enthusiasts, fishermen, rock climbers, hikers, bicyclists and hunters. Locals refer to the Youghiogheny River as "the Yawk," and it is a tributary of the Monongahela River. The river's origin is in Preston County, West Virginia, near the town of Aurora, and it works its way into Garrett County, Maryland, and then into southwestern Pennsylvania. The river's name translates to "contrary river" from the Lenape language, the tongue of a Native tribe that disappeared in the 1600s with the arrival of white settlers. The Iroquois called the area *ohuipihelle*, now Ohiopyle, which translates to "white frothy water," in reference to the waterfalls and white-tipped rapids of the river. The river itself is unusual, as it flows north rather than south. More than 1,700 miles of streams and creeks flow from the Youghiogheny River to Laurel Hill

One of several waterfalls at Ohiopyle State Park. *Courtesy of the Pennsylvania Department of Conservation and Natural Resources.*

Creek, the Little Yough River and the Indian, Jacobs and Sewickley Creeks, according to the book *Youghiogheny: An Appalachian River.*

In May 1754, Lieutenant Colonel George Washington was tasked with protecting the settlers who were building a fort at what is now the city of Pittsburgh, and he planned to reach Pittsburgh by boat over the river but found its rapids and waterfalls so difficult to maneuver that he abandoned his plans and continued his journey on foot.

Ohiopyle was a weekend destination in the 1920s for Pittsburgh residents seeking escape from the teeming, smoke-filled and dirty city. For $1.65, the Baltimore and Ohio Railroad transported tourists on Sundays to Ohiopyle, where they enjoyed picnics, idyllic afternoons walking along the boardwalks near the waterfalls, dances in the pavilions, tennis games or hikes along mountain trails in the dense forest. The train left every Sunday at 8:45 a.m. and returned to Pittsburgh by 8:15 p.m.

The region was populated by farms, small businesses, coal mines, sawmills and the railroad. The demand for coke for steel production created a string of thirteen thousand coke ovens that dotted the landscape. As Ohiopyle prospered, stores, liveries and businesses opened as its population grew to more than eight hundred. The village was originally named Falls City, but its name was changed in 1891. During World War II, more than twenty-five thousand miners worked in Fayette County, but by the 1950s, the number was reduced to eleven thousand.

Today, Ohiopyle is tiny. There are no stop signs or red lights in the town. Its population was fifty-nine when recorded in the 2010 census, but this number swells to the thousands during the summer with outdoor enthusiasts eager to challenge the river's churning rapids. When Wable was a boy, Ohiopyle hadn't yet become the rafting destination it is today. This change occurred when Lance Martin started a commercial business out of a hobby by opening the first whitewater rafting company in 1959. It drew three hundred customers in its first year by using surplus military rafts.

William Wable was a coal miner. He and his wife, Louise, raised a family of three daughters and two sons on a fifty-acre farm. The family's roots in

Fayette County are deep and date to the nineteenth century, when John Wesley Wable's great-grandfather Jerimiah Wable was born in 1820. William Wable's grandfather Lucian was born in 1858, and his father was born in 1894, according to genealogical records at the National Archives. Wable was a petty thief, burglar and pickpocket turned serial killer. He was described in newspapers as a hick who grew up in the backwoods of southwestern Pennsylvania. He was a callow, reckless youth with an unsavory reputation for having sticky fingers who was kicked out of the army for stealing from fellow soldiers.

John Wesley Wable was a nomad. He ran away from home once as a child and grew into a petty thief during high school. He joined the U.S. Army but spent most of his short enlistment in the brig and was dishonorably discharged after eighteen months. "They all listened to their mom and dad except John," said his mother, Louise Wable, during a 1951 interview with the *Pittsburgh Press*. "He always had a mind of his own and wouldn't pay us any attention."

Wable attended a one-room schoolhouse, and every Sunday, he walked three miles to a small, white, wooden church for services and Sunday school, according to a story in the *Latrobe Bulletin*. He graduated from high school and floated between Ohiopyle, Cleveland, Niagara Falls and Canada after getting kicked out of the army. "He was always traveling up to his uncle's in Niagara Falls or most anywhere," said his mother. "He even went up to Canada for a while."

"John was always in trouble, but I never believed the kid would turn into a killer," said his brother Robert. "All the evidence seems to point to him. All of us had good records at Ohiopyle High School except John. He was too light-fingered and always picking up something," his brother told the *Pittsburgh Press*.

Wable was stationed at Fort Dix in New Jersey, and Robert Wable said his brother came home frequently, making the nearly three-hundred-mile trip by hitchhiking. "He often rode home by way of the turnpike from New York and New Jersey. He'd go to truck terminals and hitch rides with truckers."

Wable was restless. He did odd jobs. Newspapers described him as a farmhand. In Cleveland, he worked as a security guard and factory worker but bounced from one job to another, seeking better pay. "He'd quit one job to take another if he could make fifty cents more," said his mother.

After Wable was released from jail in Uniontown, police suspected he knew he was a wanted man after he boasted to his cellmate, Welch, that he was the Turnpike Killer. He decided to remain in the region because he knew

The Fayette County Prison in Uniontown, where Wable was briefly jailed and then released before authorities learned he was the Turnpike Killer. *Courtesy of Fayette County.*

the forest trails and the trout streams along the Youghiogheny River. Before Welch was released from jail, he told prison officials about the conversation he had with Wable, and they, in turn, notified state police. Pennsylvania State Police detectives John Cherin and Frank McKetta questioned Welch about the conversation and examined the rental car Wable failed to return after it was recovered by the rental company. Fayette County district attorney Fred Brothers also questioned Welch about Wable's boasts and said, "His story rings true."

Wable had shown an unusual interest in Welch and called the jail three times to find out when Welch would be released. Warden Jack L. Cochrane suspected Wable was planning to kill Welch. "It sounds to me like he was interested in getting him up in the mountains and getting rid of him," Cochrane said. "I think [Wable] was sorry he shot off his mouth off and wanted to get Welch out of the way."

State police suspected Wable was hiding in the Ohiopyle area after a cabin owner reported that his dwelling had been broken into and that a police radio was missing. Police believed Wable was monitoring the manhunt using the stolen radio and was able to stay a step ahead of them. Investigators also found a trail of empty food cans inside the cabin, indicating that someone was hungry when the cabin was burglarized. State police had Wable's Ohiopyle home under surveillance. "We have men at a good many spots looking for him," state police captain Jack Dodson said, according to the *Pittsburgh Post-Gazette*. Fayette County jail warden Jack Cochrane also believed Wable was still hiding somewhere in the region.

"I expect Wable will be captured before the weekend is over, and when he is captured, we expect him to confess. I think he's afraid to make a move from this area. Wable isn't the type of man who would give up a fight once police knew where he was. We learned definitely that Wable was around here because prisoners who knew him in jail saw him in Uniontown this week and called to him," reported the *Pittsburgh Sun-Telegraph*. Robert Maust and George Pastorius had been in the Fayette County Jail at the same time as Wable, reported the *Uniontown Morning Herald*.

After an $11,000 reward was announced by the American Trucking Associations and Teamsters Union, police were inundated with more than one thousand tips from individuals who claimed they had seen Wable in Philadelphia; Baltimore; Washington, D.C.; Buffalo, New York; Niagara Falls; Morgantown, West Virginia; and Erie, Pennsylvania. He was seen driving a car while disguised as a soldier. Another report said he was seen while buying ammunition in a hardware store. Police in Alice, Texas, held a man who resembled Wable for six days before releasing him before a wanted poster with a detailed description of Wable arrived. The man who resembled Wable claimed to be from Anderson, Indiana, but police there said they could not find anybody by that name.

Pennsylvania State Police issued an alert after a truck driver picked up a hitchhiker fitting Wable's description in East Liverpool, Ohio, and drove him to Pittsburgh. Police in the Philadelphia area also claimed they saw Wable. When police pulled up to the man in the Philadelphia suburb of Wynnewood, the man "jumped as if shot." "You scared me," the man replied before fleeing on foot through a used car lot, according to the *Pittsburgh Sun-Telegraph*. Baltimore police claimed a vagrant matching Wable's physical characteristics was seen asking for directions to Baltimore. In Cleveland, a used car dealer claimed Wable took a 1950 Mercury for a test drive and never returned, leaving a stolen Buick in its place.

Despite the different sightings of Wable, he remained in Fayette County. He walked into Beeson's Lunchroom in Uniontown around midnight on September 30 and asked owner Theodore Chesler if he could borrow a screwdriver to fix his car, which had broken down on the street outside of his business. "I loaned him a screwdriver, and we went out to an old Chevy, but we couldn't get it started," said Chesler. "I offered to call AAA, but the fellow said he'd sleep in the car all night and get help in the morning. I went back inside, and an hour later, my car, my screwdriver and the young fellow were all missing. I practically helped Wable steal it," Chesler told the *Pittsburgh Press.*

Wable drove the stolen car to Cleveland to see his girlfriend, Leora Crissey, but he was confronted by her mother and stepfather, who told Wable they had turned the gun over to police. The color rushed from Wable's face. "He turned white. His appetite wasn't so good after that," Jandura told the *Pittsburgh Sun-Telegraph.*

Jandura and his wife, Elsie, were suspicious and wondered where Wable had gotten the money he needed to live on since he had recently quit his job at Parker Appliance Co. "I wanted to know how he was making a living, and he said he was pushing counterfeit money," Jandura said. "He told us he had three jobs to go to and couldn't make up his mind which one to take. He was vague about the jobs. I asked him to leave. I thought it would help him make up his mind about the jobs. Wable implied he was in trouble, but we didn't know what it was." Wable asked Jandura to return the gun. "I told him the place was searched and the police took it." Elsie Jandura ordered Wable to stay away from her daughter until he found a job. "You can't see Leora anymore until you get a job and straighten out. Don't come back till you can prove you're working by showing a paycheck."

Cleveland homicide detectives questioned Crissey about the gun. "Did Wable own a gun?" asked detectives. "Certainly. He always carried a gun," she replied, according to an account in the *Cleveland Plain Dealer.* Wable was in a panic. Police had the murder weapon and matched the bullets fired from the gun through ballistic tests to the murders of Pitts and Woodward and the wounding of Shephard. Wable was driving a stolen car, which he realized police were searching for, and he recalled the foolish, incriminating statement he made to Charlie Welch while in the Fayette County Jail—it was coming back to haunt him. After leaving Crissey's home, Wable spent the night in a tourist camp outside Cleveland. The next day, he hit the road for California.

6

ON THE RUN

Marvin Parson had just completed U.S. Army bootcamp in California and was headed to see his wife in Oklahoma before continuing to Fort Bragg, North Carolina. The twenty-year-old soldier was traveling with a friend, J.D. Francis, seventeen, when their car broke down in Clear Creek, about 245 miles from Bakersfield. Parson called his family, asking for money to pay for repairs, but after waiting for two days, no money arrived, so Parson and Francis hitched a ride on the outskirts of the Mojave Desert on October 12 with a young man who was driving a blue Chevrolet.

John Wesley Wable had driven to California after leaving Cleveland and was traveling east when he picked up the two hitchhikers. He was running out of money for gas and food and drove his passengers through Gallup, Grants and Los Lunas, New Mexico, before stopping for gas at the Whiting Brothers Gas station on Route 66 outside of Albuquerque. Parson was asleep in the back seat. Wable urged Francis to walk into the gas station office and grab the cash from the register while he distracted the attendant, twelve-year-old Andrew Guttierrez, by asking him to check the car's oil. When Francis came back to the car, Wable yelled, "Let's get the hell out of here!" according to an account of the holdup in the *Albuquerque Journal*.

As Wable sped away, Guttierrez's father, Hijinio, the station's manager, arrived and chased the vehicle before giving up, because his son was alone in the station. "If my older boy, Hijinio Jr., had been there, he might have tried to stop the robbers. And he might have gotten hurt. I'm glad things

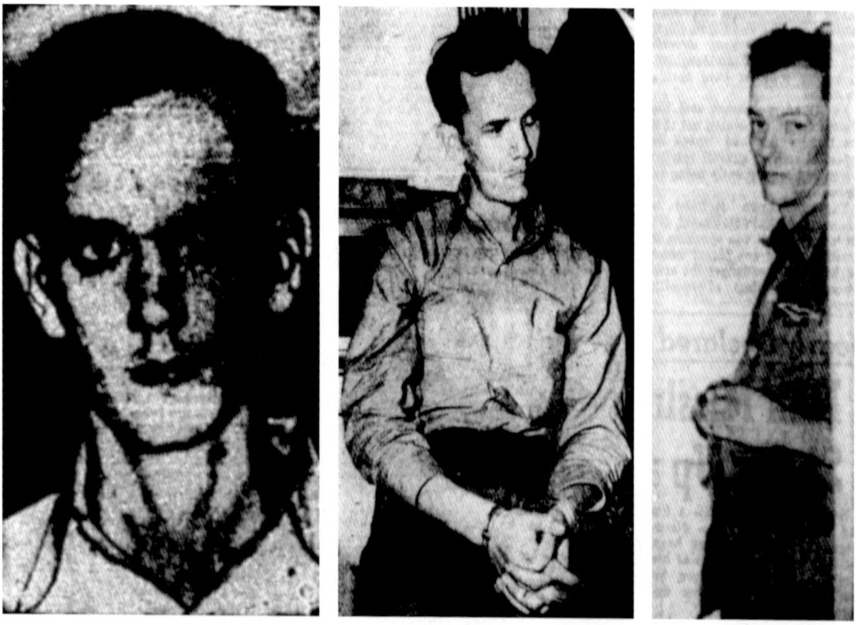

A photograph of Wable following his arrest in New Mexico. From left to right: *Wire service photograph,* New York Daily News *and* Pittsburgh Post-Gazette.

happened the way they did. The main thing is nobody got hurt," Guttierrez told the *Albuquerque Journal.*

New Mexico state troopers T.J. Chavez and B.E. Lucas set up roadblocks on both sides of the Rio Grande, while Belen police sergeant Valentine Torres drove his cruiser to a nearby railroad overpass. Torres saw Wable's blue sedan speeding toward him, so Torres turned on his emergency lights and headed directly for Wable, who led police on a thirty-mile chase from Bernalillo County into neighboring Valencia County, reaching speeds of one hundred miles per hour. Wable avoided a head-on collision with Torres's cruiser by swerving into the parking lot of the 85 Courts Motel, jumping out of the car and fleeing on foot while Torres arrested Parson and Francis. The young men were shocked to learn Wable was the target of a nationwide manhunt. "You're kidding! We thought he was just trying to beat a speeding ticket," Parson said. "We didn't even know his name," reported the *Albuquerque Journal.*

Caroline Smith, a twenty-three-year-old nurse at the hospital in Belen, and a friend, Midge Harman, twenty, were going to see a movie when they saw the police roadblock. Smith asked an officer she knew about what was happening, and he told her about the holdup. "I didn't know who [Wable] was at the time. I just knew he was a man wanted for robbery in Albuquerque," Smith said. "We were so excited. We never did get to the movie," she told the *Albuquerque Journal*.

The two women had a hunch. If they were trying to evade capture by the police, they would head for the Jarales Crossing, a busy railroad intersection and homeless encampment frequented by transients who were trying to jump on passing trains. "He'll make for the railway," Harman thought. They drove along the dirt road leading to Jarales and saw Wable trying to hitch a ride. He was walking fast and occasionally turning around at oncoming cars. "We knew him by his blue shirt and brown pants," Smith said.

The women drove past Wable, then circled and passed him a second time before alerting police to Wable's location. "We thought he might have a gun, but I didn't want to find out," Harman said. "If I had known he was the Phantom Killer, I would have turned pea green and purple," added Smith. "He was pretty teed off at us. He gave us several you-go-to-heck looks."

He was seen running through a field but made the mistake of doubling back to try to retrieve his car. Police cornered Wable, who surrendered quietly. Authorities didn't realize Wable was wanted for murder until they checked on the ownership of the vehicle he was driving and discovered it was stolen—and that Wable was wanted for two murders in Pennsylvania.

Wable was lodged in the Bernalillo County Jail and placed in a four-by-eight-foot cell, where a crowd of police, sheriff deputies, reporters, photographers and the curious huddled around Wable as he sat next to Undersheriff Walter Geis, a native of Pittsburgh who had moved to New Mexico, and District Attorney Paul Tackett. Authorities allowed a crowd of onlookers to enter the cellblock and witness Geiss interrogate Wable. Wable was dirty, tired, hungry and haggard-looking and asked his jailers for a cigarette and the opportunity to take a shower. "You'll get one as soon as we're through," Geis told him. "Now, that guy you bought the watch from, how much did it cost you?" Geis asked. "Twenty-eight bucks. It was an Elgin," Wable replied.

Police learned that after leaving Cleveland, Wable had driven through Oklahoma and Texas before reaching Bakersfield, California. Bernalillo County sheriff Harold Hubbell said authorities had no idea Wable was the target of a nationwide manhunt when they arrested him, but that didn't stop Hubbell from mistakenly concluding that Parson and Francis were also involved in the turnpike murders. He erroneously claimed that Parson and Francis knew "a lot about those turnpike murders. They apparently had been operating as a trio for some time."

Belen is a small town thirty-five miles south of Albuquerque along the Rio Grande in Valencia County, which stretches from the Sandia Mountains to the Arizona border. The name translated from Spanish means "Our Lady of Bethlehem." In July 1945, sections of the first atomic bomb dropped on Japan were trucked through Belen on their way to the Trinity test site at what is now known as the White Sands Missile Range. The town's claim to fame is that it was the home of William F. Beaver, who invented the waffle fry after designing a machine to cut potatoes into waffle-like slices.

Wable played cat and mouse with photographers who were trying to take his photograph as he sat in a cell. Every time a photographer tried to snap Wable's photograph, he placed his right hand over his face—but he was less publicity shy than he seemed. He claimed he didn't know that his photograph had been plastered in newspapers across the country and tried to barter with reporters for a copy of the editions containing stories of his capture. For a man who said he would not talk, he kept answering questions from anybody who asked. "This is my first visit to Albuquerque, and I don't like the place," he told the *Albuquerque Journal*.

Geis began questioning Wable. "Do you have any guns? Any foreign ones?" Geis asked. "I had a couple of guns…a .22 and a .32," said Wable. "What happened to them?" Geis continued. "I dunno. I got no idea where they are."

Geis then asked Wable about the pocket watch he had taken from Shepard after attacking him. "I hocked the watch," Wable said. "Sure, I don't know what I got for it. The pawn ticket's in my billfold downstairs. I didn't take it from any truck driver. I bought it from a certain fellow, and I think he is the Phantom Killer. I never knew they were hunting me because I didn't kill anybody." "Who'd you get it from?" Geis continued. "Some guy on the street…downtown Cleveland around Fifth Street." Wable hesitated for a moment when Geis asked him to describe the man who sold him the pocket watch and then claimed someone else had killed the truck drivers. "I'm not saying [the name], but I think I know the man. I'll get him. I got friends who'll get him, but I'm not saying who he is until I get back to Pennsylvania. I'm not guilty. Just cold and tired. I didn't kill anybody. Yeah, I heard about the turnpike killings. My girl told me, but I won't tell you her name either."

Wable said he left Cleveland because of "woman troubles" and claimed he was unaware that he was a wanted man and the target of a nationwide manhunt—even though he seemed upset when he learned that police had recovered the murder weapon. He was held in solitary confinement because he threatened to kill himself. His jailers took his clothes, forcing him to sit naked while shivering in the cold on a cell bunk. "I told them if I'm ever found guilty of any kind of murder, then I'd kill myself. I'd hang myself. I didn't mean I'd kill myself now. I'm innocent. I don't know anything about any gun."

Wable's mother, Louise, couldn't believe her son was a killer. "I can't believe within myself that he would do what they're saying. I know John was home all day July 25. That was the day of the Sunday school picnic. John did not want to go. He stayed home until dark and then went to a nearby Dinner Bell. He came home later that night," she said, according to the *Pittsburgh Press.* "It's a great relief to me to know he is in police custody and alive. His dad and I still insist that he had nothing to do with the turnpike killings. Maybe now, he will prove he had nothing to do with the turnpike killings," she told the *Uniontown Morning Herald.*

Wable's capture triggered a mad scramble for the $11,000 reward. Caroline Smith didn't know that a bounty had been offered and felt uncomfortable with the attention she was receiving from journalists. "We've done nothing about the reward," she said. "All we know is what the newspapers stated and what a Pittsburgh newspaper reporter told us over the telephone. I feel like I'm on exhibition. Everybody looks at us all the time. And everybody's talking. No one knows what's going on," she told the *Roswell Daily Record.*

7

THE CONFESSION

Westmoreland County assistant district attorney Joseph Loughran learned of Wable's capture and immediately made plans to fly from Pittsburgh to New Mexico with county detective Merle Musick and state police corporal William Smith. The trio had worked together before, investigating the murder of a payroll clerk at a local brickyard in 1952. Loughran obtained a conviction, and the gunman died in the electric chair. Loughran's boss, Westmoreland County district attorney Alexander Sculco, had already decided he would seek the death penalty for Wable.

Sculco was a product of the Westmoreland County Democratic Party political machine that was under the thumb of organized crime, which had controlled western Pennsylvania for decades. He served as an assistant prosecutor before being elected district attorney, and he later became a judge. Sculco had ties to brothers Samuel and Gabriel Mannarino, who were placed on the FBI's Top Hoodlum list as two of the top Mafia bosses in the nation. The Mafia dominated county government and politics by bribing judges, police and elected officials, according to declassified FBI records at the National Archives documenting the history of organized crime in western Pennsylvania.

The Westmoreland County District Attorney's Office, as well as Judge Edward Bauer, were controlled by the Mannarinos, whose payoffs protected their organization from police raids. Clandestine gambling casinos operated throughout the county, raking in millions of dollars a year. Bookie joints and horse parlors operated within the shadow of the courthouse. Prostitution flourished. Bookies operated openly and used local police officers as chauffeurs to pick up the day's gambling proceeds. Judges, police chiefs, prosecutors and elected officials were compromised by the mob. Election fraud was rampant. FBI records documented the ties between elected officials and the Mafia, not only in Westmoreland County but throughout western Pennsylvania. Racketeers were seldom arrested. Convicted bookmakers were treated leniently.

While jury selection was underway in the Wable trial, a federal grand jury in Pittsburgh indicted thirty-eight people, seventeen from Westmoreland County, for election fraud stemming from the 1952 election. Dead men and women left their graves on election day and voted, "once, twice, thrice…and make no mistake, these phantom votes and absentees do swing elections," reported the *Pittsburgh Post-Gazette*. One man cast a ballot even though he spent election day in the county jail.

Collier's Weekly published an exposé in 1950 titled "Something's Rotten in the State of Pennsylvania" that detailed the unholy alliance between the Mafia and political figures. It revealed how the rackets dominated politics and law enforcement and focused on Judge Edward Bauer and Sculco. A ministerial group formed Operation Crusade and launched a campaign to rid the county of corruption, targeting Bauer, who presided at the Wable trial, and his fellow judges, Richard Laird and John O'Connell.

Operation Crusade singled out Bauer for ignoring corruption, his tolerance for gambling and the light sentences he imposed on racketeers. The ministers were critical of Sculco because of his failure to arrest and prosecute organized crime figures. His chief detective, Howard "Buddy" Turner, served as the bagman for mobsters, according to FBI reports. Turner became a detective in 1939, despite having no previous law enforcement experience and a criminal record for sex offenses.

The Westmoreland County Courthouse is located in the City of Greensburg, which sits at the foothills of the Laurel Highlands. The town was named by veterans who served under Revolutionary War general Nathanael Greene of Rhode Island. The county once encompassed the entire corner of southwestern Pennsylvania before it was divided into several counties. Westmoreland was a mixture of industrial cities, like New Kensington in the north, Jeannette in the center and Monessen in the south. The grit and grime of these steel- and glass-making towns contrasted with the rolling hills, mountains, streams and the estates of the lush Ligonier Valley to the east. The valley has been home to some of Pittsburgh's wealthiest industrialists, such as the Mellon family. Richard Beatty Mellon founded the exclusive Rolling Rock Club, a rich man's hideaway and hunting, fishing and shooting preserve. Richard King Mellon was a behind-the-scenes political power in Pittsburgh and was a force behind Pittsburgh's renaissance in the late 1950s that transformed Pittsburgh from a dirty, smokey city into an urban centerpiece.

Westmoreland County has a rich history. The Whiskey Rebellion was fought in Westmoreland, Allegheny, Fayette and Washington Counties in 1794. The Bushy Run Battlefield near Greensburg was a site of a decisive British victory during the French and Indian War in 1763. Fort Ligonier to the east in Ligonier overlooks Loyalhanna Creek and was a vital supply link for British forces during the war. Hanna's Town, located outside of Greensburg, was the first county seat and site of the first English court west of the Allegheny Mountains. Industrialist Henry Clay Frick was born in West Overton in the southern end of the county, and Judge Thomas Mellon, the patriarch of the wealthy Mellon family, lived in the county at one time.

Wable waived extradition to Pennsylvania, so Loughran flew back to Pittsburgh while Musick and Smith returned to Greensburg with Wable by train, traveling from Albuquerque on the Atchison, Topeka and Santa Fe Railway's *Super Chief* to Chicago and then took the Pennsylvania Railroad's *Liberty Limited* to Greensburg. The detectives kept Wable sequestered in a Pullman drawing room as the train chugged through New Mexico, Colorado, Kansas and Missouri before crossing into Illinois on its way to Chicago. He was quiet during the early hours of the journey until Musick asked him if he wanted to talk about the turnpike killings. "You wouldn't believe me if I told you," Wable replied. Without any prodding from Musick, Wable said he didn't kill anybody and blamed the killings on another man, a mysterious Jim Parks. Musick asked Wable if he wanted to tell his side of the story, so after dinner, Wable began writing a fourteen-page statement in pencil as the *Super Chief* passed through Dodge City, Kansas, and Galesburg, Illinois.

Wable was not represented by an attorney following his arrest in New Mexico and did not have any attorney to advise him before he signed the document, although he was warned by the detectives that anything he said would be used against him at a trial. It wasn't until 1966 that the U.S. Supreme Court ruled in *Miranda v. Arizona* that a person in police custody has the right to remain silent and have an attorney present when they are questioned by police. Wable wrote that he gave the statement freely, "without any threats or promises. I wrote this of my own free will and was treated wonderfully by officers and [they] didn't promise me anything," reported the *Pittsburgh Press.*

Wable identified Jim Parks as the killer. He said he met Parks at a downtown Pittsburgh Greyhound bus station after returning from Cleveland in June 1953. Parks approached Wable with an offer to make some easy money by circulating counterfeit cash at bars and taverns. Wable described details of the killings, which he attributed to Parks.

> *Around Irwin,* [Pennsylvania], *he saw this truck setting by itself. He* [Parks] *said to drive on by real slow then to come back around. We did then he got out and took the .32 with him and told me to come back and get him later. I saw an accident on the road down the way about one mile from there and stopped to look at it when I heard the shot.*

Wable was referring to the six-vehicle car accident that killed two people and injured seven. The accident occurred between four cars and two tractor trailer trucks on a fog-shrouded section of the turnpike. Traffic was clogged for miles. One of the victims was trapped in the vehicle and burned to death.

> *I turned and went back up the hill and picked him up, just like he was hitchhiking. He gave me the gun and said to turn around and get going. I wanted to stop and look at the accident, but he said not to—somebody may see us. Jim was looking for a truck off by itself so he could shoot the driver. We saw many trucks but none by themselves. That was the first and only one that night.*

Parks and Wable took a drive on the turnpike on July 25, when they saw Woodward's truck as they neared the Irwin Interchange. He said Parks was searching for a truck parked by itself because he wanted to shoot the driver. They drove up and down the turnpike for two hours until traffic eased up, and Parks ordered Wable to stop. Wable pulled off the highway, Parks got out, then came back. As they drove away, Wable said he glanced at the truck and saw the body lying on the front seat.

Wable's handwritten confession was interrupted by dinner as the train entered the former Wild West frontier town of Dodge City, Kansas. Wable resumed writing on October 15 as the train passed through Galesburg, Illinois, the home of poet Carl Sandburg and television's Superman George Reeves. On July 31, Wable said he and Parks got off the turnpike at the New

Stanton Interchange and took Route 40 to Washington, Pennsylvania, then followed Route 18 and Route 30 toward Liverpool, Ohio, and then headed for Lisbon, where they saw John Shepard's truck on Green's Hill. Parks took the gun and got out of the car while Wable drove on to Lisbon before he turned around and returned to the point where he left Parks.

> *I was driving by the truck when the driver flagged me down. I stopped, and he told me that he thought he had busted an artery in his head. I told him I would go back and get an ambulance for him. He gave me a five-dollar bill and told me to buy gas with it when I went back up the road. Jim got in, and I told him he didn't kill the driver. He gave me hell and asked me what I said to him. I told him then he told me he would fix him for good. He took the car and left me standing along the road. When he came back, I thought he had finished him off, but I know different now. He had a pair of pants with him. I pawned the watch in a Cleveland hock shop. It was an Elgin pocket watch. I got ten dollars for it to take Leora out that night. I would never pass counterfeit money when she was around so she would not be charged in the racket.…I left for California because Leora and I had a few words, and I told her I would never see her again.*

The train pulled into Dearborn Station in Chicago, where a half-dozen photographers were waiting for Wable, Musick and Smith. As the handcuffed Wable got off the train, he crouched and tried to hide his face when he saw the photographers and was on the verge of tears when Smith and Musick escorted him to a waiting Chicago police car. Corporal Smith offered Wable a cigarette to calm his nerves. Then Chicago police drove them two miles to the Union Station to catch the *Liberty Limited* to Greensburg.

Wable was met in Greensburg by Sculco, Loughran, state police major Andrew Hudock, a half-dozen state troopers, Westmoreland County sheriff Howard "Bud" Thomas and Greensburg police officers, along with reporters and photographers. "I haven't seen you for a while," quipped Loughran. "That's for sure," Wable replied. "How was your trip?" asked Loughran. Wable was hustled off to Alderman Henry Fredrickson's office for arraignment on two counts of murder. Wable's confession was front-page news throughout the region and the country.

Pittsburgh and Greensburg newspapers heralded his confession and the introduction of a mystery man into the mix, but authorities believed Wable was the killer. "He has implicated himself in all three shootings," said state police captain Jack Dodson. "He wrote it all by himself. We have little doubt that Wable is in this alone. At the present time, we are not looking for anyone else. He may claim that another man pulled the trigger, but our information just won't support that. We know Wable from way back, and he usually works alone," Dodson told the *Pittsburgh Press*. "We are still checking his [original statement] and we believe there is no other man. Give us a few hours, and we may break him. He has shed no tears and shows no remorse," Sculco added.

At Wable's arraignment before Frederickson, Sculco asked Wable whether he realized Parks was out looking to kill someone when they entered the turnpike.

"Did you give him the gun used in the shootings?" Sculco asked Wable.

"Yes, but I didn't know what he was going to do with it. I drove away and heard a shot. Then I drove back and picked him up. The next day, he gave me $500 to keep it for him—half of it in counterfeit money."

Wable was hustled off to the state police headquarters, where John Shepard, the man who had come face to face with Wable on the turnpike the night he was shot, was unable to identify Wable as the gunman. Shepard remembered the light-colored car the man was driving and his feminine-sounding voice. Wable later took investigators to the turnpike and pointed out the exact spots where he said Parks had shot Pitts and Woodward. Wable was housed in the Westmoreland County Jail, a brick and granite structure located behind the courthouse. The jail was an ominous-looking building with a large clock tower hovering above the entrance. Prisoners are now housed in a modern facility located several miles south of Greensburg.

Wable was placed in an eight-foot-square cell and watched around the clock, as one guard was stationed outside his cell to prevent Wable from dying by suicide. A second guard checked on Wable every fifteen minutes, noted his behavior and tracked the amount of time Wable slept, when he awoke, when he washed, when he ate and whenever he walked back and forth in his cell, according to the *Patriot News* in Harrisburg. "Although he smokes, he is not visibly nervous," noted a guard. When his mother and sister visited him, the guard wrote that Wable told the women, "He is not the triggerman."

8

THE RECKONING

The murder trial of John Wesley Wable began on the frigid, snowy morning of March 1, 1954, with jury selection in the Westmoreland County Courthouse in Greensburg, about thirty-five miles southeast of Pittsburgh. An overnight rain had changed to snow, blanketing roads and highways with five inches of ice that made driving treacherous. The temperature the previous day was fifty-eight degrees Fahrenheit, but the temperature dropped to twelve degrees Fahrenheit by morning, as high winds created a blinding snow squall that reduced highway visibility and turned local roads into ice rinks.

The four-story courthouse was built in 1906 and was an architectural mix of Greek, Roman and Renaissance styles known as Beaux-Arts. The dome of the four-story building rose 175 feet above the sidewalk and was adorned with ornamental gold- and ivory-colored terra cotta. To get into the courthouse, visitors entered from Main Street beneath a rounded arch and ornamental carvings and figurines. Above the entrance were three female figures characterizing justice, law and the people. Corinthian columns adorned the ground floor, with blocks of flower-shaped designs known as rosettes embedded in the ceilings. The floors of the building were composed of small colored tiles. Bronze railings adorned the grand staircase leading to the upper floors, which were finished in mahogany and white oak.

Wable's family braved the snow and cold, driving thirty-seven icy miles from the mountainous Ohiopyle area to Greensburg. The roads were so icy that eighteen people who were summoned for jury duty, along with

The exterior of the Westmoreland County Courthouse in Greensburg. *From Wikipedia.*

chief defense attorney A.C. Scales, were late for court, according to the *Pittsburgh Press.* William and Louise Wable, along with their son, Robert, and daughters, Betty Marmie and Ruby Wable, were barred by sheriff deputies from entering the courtroom because Judge Edward Bauer refused to allow the public inside during jury selection. "My boy didn't do it," said William Wable. "Whoever did it must have been crazy, must have been out of his mind entirely. My boy is innocent," added Louise Wable. "I don't think he did it," said his brother, Robert. He also said John "feels pretty good" and is in "awfully good spirits," according to a reporter for the *Pittsburgh Sun-*

A photograph of the dome of the Westmoreland County Courthouse. *Courtesy of Westmoreland County.*

Telegraph. The trip was difficult for Louise Wable, who was suffering from a brain tumor. "Mother is in no condition to stand this, "Robert added. "She's had several brain tumor operations in the last couple of years."

Wable had not been represented by an attorney since his arrest in New Mexico on October 12, so when District Attorney Alexander Sculco announced he would seek the death penalty against Wable, Judge Richard Laird appointed a three-man defense team to him. In addition to A.C. Scales, a veteran attorney who had been practicing law for more than two decades, Laird selected two young lawyers, B. Patrick Costello and Richard McCormick, to assist the defense. Costello and McCormick would not have been qualified to defend Wable today under the standards set by the American Bar Association and the State of Pennsylvania. In Pennsylvania, a minimum of five years of trial experience is required before a lawyer can defend a client in a capital case. The defense attorneys must also have been the lead or cocounsel in eight significant jury trials.

Arvel C. Scales grew up dirt poor on a farm near Evansville, Indiana, according to his son, attorney John Scales, a former state senator and district attorney. Arvel Scales was raised by David and Martha Sparks after his parents died. He rode a mule six miles to school every day and sold watermelons during the summer to earn money. During summer vacations in college, Scales sold Bibles in the Monongahela Valley of southwestern Pennsylvania before graduating from Indiana University. He attended the university's law school for two years before spending his final year at Georgetown, where he graduated.

He returned to selling Bibles during the Great Depression. Eventually, he was hired to teach history at a high school in the small town of Pitcairn outside of Pittsburgh. When one of his female students complained about a grade she received, he said he couldn't change the grade but offered her an alternative. "How about I marry you instead?" She agreed, provided they wait until she finished high school, according to his son.

John Scales said the defense team had an uphill battle before them, since Wable had signed an incriminating account of the crimes on the train ride from New Mexico. It would be the defense's job to discredit the statement by arguing that it was coerced from Wable or that he was unaware of his rights. "There was no way to win from a defense standpoint," said Scales. "He did what he could. He was a damn good lawyer."

B. Patrick Costello joined the navy in 1942 after graduating from high school and became a fighter pilot. He later graduated from Notre Dame and the University of Pennsylvania's law school. McCormick had "read" the law under the tutelage of his father and uncle before attending law school at the University of Pittsburgh for a year and passing the bar exam. For their efforts, the three lawyers were each paid $333.33 by the county.

Assistant District Attorneys Joe Loughran and John Best would prosecute Wable. Loughran was a skilled prosecutor who had been in the district attorney's office since 1946 and had been an attorney since 1931. In 1952, he sent Joseph Phillips to the electric chair for killing a payroll clerk during a botched holdup. Loughran was also a member of the political machine that controlled the county. He once charged a Westmoreland County election official with tampering with public records after she gave the FBI copies of the voting record of Mafia boss Dominick Anzalone, who was not a U.S. citizen and therefore ineligible to vote. The government was trying to deport Anzalone as an undesirable immigrant because of his mob connections. Best also was a veteran prosecutor who was hired as an assistant to then–district attorney Edward Bauer. Best served in the U.S. Army Air Force during World War II and spent twenty-five years working as a prosecutor.

Ironically, Scales and Loughran were once partners in a small law firm until Loughran left to become a county prosecutor. Despite their past relationship, the two sparred during a contentious jury selection process characterized by sharp arguments between the two men. Judge Bauer warned both sides to control their tempers. "Gentlemen, you've got a long way to go. I wish you would do your best to keep your tempers."

The defense opposed several potential jurors—four were truck drivers—and after six hours of questioning, the two sides could agree on only three jurors. Sculco accused the defense of employing stalling tactics by raising issues that should have been taken care of months before. Scales wanted the murder weapon tested independently and for Wable to undergo an examination by a psychiatrist chosen by the defense. "We granted them ample time to present their case, and now, in the middle of picking a jury, they want to check this gun. I think they are doing everything possible to delay the trial. We are bending over backwards to give the defendant a break."

Scales accused Sculco of trying to stack the jury with death penalty proponents. "If anyone is stalling, it's the state. The figures speak for themselves. Look how many veniremen we have accepted and the state has turned down," said Scales, according to the *Pittsburgh Sun-Telegraph*. "This is the most difficult [jury selection] I've seen in my twenty-five years as a member of the bar."

The jury selection process is known as voir dire, meaning to "speak the truth," and is meant to screen potential jurors who may harbor a bias against the accused. Attorneys question each person about the case, asking such questions as, "What have you read about the crime? Would that affect your deliberations? Would you give more credence to a police officer over another witness? Have you ever been a victim of a crime? Do you have relatives in law enforcement? Would you be willing to apply the law as the judge instructs during your deliberations? Could you condemn a man to death based on circumstantial evidence?" Jurors must also be willing to forgo reading newspapers or listening to radio or television broadcasts about the case during their service.

One man said he would be reluctant to vote for a death sentence. "You would hesitate to find the death penalty in a case involving circumstantial evidence?" Costello asked. "I would, but if the person openly admits the crime, of course, he writes his own ticket as far as I'm concerned," reported the *Pittsburgh Post-Gazette*. The most critical question was if Wable was found guilty of first-degree murder, would a juror impose the death sentence. One man said he was morally opposed to capital punishment. "Is it a matter of conscience?" Loughran asked. "Yes, it is," the man replied before he was excused. A minister said he favored the death penalty, but "being a minister, I couldn't be party to it," recounted the *Pittsburgh Post-Gazette*.

It was obvious during the selection process that some individuals didn't want to serve on the jury. One woman told Judge Bauer that she was too nervous to serve, but Bauer advised her to "try to relax," according to the *Pittsburgh Press.* Another individual was concerned about the length of the trial. "How long would I have to stay here, three or four weeks? I wouldn't want to stay that long."

The selection process exhausted the 213-member jury pool until it was whittled down to handful due to the challenges each side was invoking to excuse jurors they didn't like. The defense rejected 22 jury members for cause and another 22 were excused on preemptory challenges without specifying a reason. So few potential jurors remained that Bauer ordered Sheriff Howard Thomas to send his deputies into the streets of municipalities during a snow squall to shanghai people for jury duty, according to the *Pittsburgh Press.* William Larimer made the mistake of stopping for a moment to browse in the window of a store near the courthouse when Sheriff Thomas snagged him. The twelve jurors and two alternatives were finally selected. The panel was composed of a crane operator, a coal miner, a telephone solicitor for an insurance company, an electroplater, a machinist, a steel worker, housewives and several unemployed individuals.

As soon as the seven men and five women were seated, the trial suffered another setback when Ronald Todd asked Bauer to be excused because his wife was about to undergo an operation and he was needed at home to care for their three children. He was replaced by an alternate.

"Why didn't you mention this before?" Bauer asked.

"Nobody asked," Todd replied.

Westmoreland County officials were worried about the cost of prosecuting Wable. The county commissioners budgeted $25,000 to install an air conditioning system in the judges' chambers the following year, but that money was eaten up by the trial. The county paid a total of $240 a day in witness fees, $168 a day to house and feed the jury, $98 a day in jurors' fees and nearly $1,000 for the defense attorneys.

Judge Bauer's courtroom was one of the largest in the courthouse. There was a balcony at the back of the courtroom to seat the public. Bauer's courtroom was one of four named after the seasons of the year. His courtroom was named the "summer courtroom," and he presided from a bench overlooking the counsel table, where opposing lawyers sat. To the judge's right was the jury box made of handmade oak spindles. Large, gilded globes covered the light bulbs suspended from the ceiling. The long benches where the public sat were also made of oak and were so highly polished with decades of varnish that an individual could see their face in the wood's reflection.

The tall, lanky Wable was escorted from the jail to the courtroom by deputies Braden Leasure, Conrad Perna and Cliff Weaver. He was clean-shaven, had a recent haircut and wore a tan suit and matching tie. He showed little interest in the jury selection process, drumming his fingers on the table, crossing and uncrossing his legs and occasionally scanning the courtroom. At the day's end, he was taken back to his cell to read his comic books, according to Warden William Hohn, who told reporters that Wable ate and slept well and attended religious services every Wednesday evening and Sunday morning but never talked to his jailers, although he mingled with other inmates during exercise periods.

9

THE TRIAL

Westmoreland County assistant district attorney John Best took just twenty-eight minutes to outline the Commonwealth of Pennsylvania's case against Wable. Best began by telling the jury that it was Wable, not some mysterious individual named Jim Parks, who killed Henry Franklin Pitts as he slept in his truck that was parked along the Pennsylvania Turnpike in 1953. Jim Parks, Best added, was a figment of Wable's imagination and a way of shifting the blame for the actual killings onto someone else who didn't exist.

"We will produce witnesses who will state that there is a series of crimes, and the state will place Wable at the scene of those crimes and show the motive," said Best, according to an account in the *Pittsburgh Post-Gazette*. He also explained to the jury that even if Wable didn't pull the trigger of the gun that killed Pitts, he was equally guilty as Parks. "If I and another man plan to commit a crime and provide him with a gun to do the deed and provide him with a car, even though I did not commit the shooting, I am equally guilty. That may come in this case."

Wable faced a jury that would determine if he was guilty or innocent. If the panel found him guilty, the jurors would then decide whether he lived or died for his crime. He needed to convince the jurors that he was merely an accomplice to the slaying and should not be executed. Even if he was acquitted of killing Pitts, he still faced trial for killing Woodward. The trial was major news in western Pennsylvania, as well as around the country.

Judge Bauer opened his seldom-used balcony of his second-floor courtroom to provide additional seating for the lines of spectators who wanted to attend the trial. Bauer had a long history as an attorney in the county and served as district attorney before being elected judge. He was a man of slight build with graying hair who sat upright on the bench and constantly had a stern expression on his face. Bauer had served in the army and was a pilot during World War I; he later graduated from law school at the University of Pittsburgh.

Sculco had no authority to try Wable for the shooting of John Shepard because that crime occurred in Ohio, but Woodward's murder and the attempted murder of Shepard would play pivotal roles in the Pennsylvania prosecution. Sculco's evidence against Wable was also stronger in the Pitts case. There was physical evidence to prove that Pitts was slain by Wable, and eyewitness evidence put Wable on the turnpike at the time of the killing. The bullets of the gun he hid in his girlfriend's Ohio home also matched the caliber of the gun used to kill Pitts and Woodward and wound Shepard.

"[The commonwealth] has amassed sufficient evidence to warrant a conviction of first-degree [murder] and send him to his death in the electric chair," continued Best. "We will prove Wable's car was on the turnpike the night of the murder. We will call a witness who will tell you that Wable confessed he was the Turnpike Killer while in jail. Witnesses will tell you how Wable got the gun and the watch which was stolen from Shepard and will tell you how Cleveland police found it in a pawnshop. It was through this watch we obtained our first clue to Wable," reported the *Monessen Daily Independent* and the *Pittsburgh Sun-Telegraph*.

Best explained to the jurors that the three crimes—the killing of Pitts and Woodward and the wounding of Shepard—were so intertwined that he could not present evidence in the Pitts case without bringing in evidence from the others to show their similarities. He also said Shepard would be a key prosecution witness, as he came face to face with Wable the night he was shot. "Mr. Shepard will be here to identify that he talked with the defendant the morning he was shot," Best said.

Judge Bauer was anxious to get the case underway and warned the jury that he would hold court from 9:00 a.m. to 5:00 p.m. and schedule a second session from 7:00 p.m. to 10:00 p.m., as well as continue the trial on Saturdays if he needed to. B. Patrick Costello delivered the opening argument for the defense with a warning from Scales: "Pat, you can open, but please don't open it so wide that I can't get it closed," recalled his son, John Scales, in an interview with the author. Costello had been practicing law for a year after graduating from the law school at the University of Pennsylvania when he was appointed to help defend Wable.

"The evidence John Wesley Wable will put into this case will not be circumstantial. It will be positive, concrete evidence. You must ask yourself: Is this the man who pulled the trigger on the gun that killed Harry Franklin Pitts? That's the only question you have to decide," Costello said.

> *I know that John Wesley Wable is getting a fair trial and is going to continue to get a fair trial from twelve men and women. He will tell you that he was born in a little village of Ohiopyle and lived there all his life. He will tell you how he grew up on his father's farm with two sisters and a brother. He'll tell you that he graduated from Ohiopyle High School and went to a little white church near his home.*
>
> *John Wesley Wable will reveal he was not on the turnpike at the time the commonwealth said he was by producing its own witnesses. And he'll bring witnesses in here to prove it. John Wesley Wable is on trial for killing Harry Franklin Pitts. Not for anyone else. I know you've been watching him. Continue to watch him. Watch him on the witness stand and ask yourself. Is that the fellow who killed Harry Franklin Pitts?*

Loughran began presenting the state's case by displaying a drawing to the jury showing the locations along the turnpike where Pitts and Woodward were killed. Pitts had pulled off the turnpike to sleep for a few hours before resuming his trip. Pitts's wife, Elizabeth, drove to Greensburg from Bowling Green, Virginia, with Joyce, her nine-year-old daughter, to testify. Elizabeth Pitts said her husband left their home and drove 125 miles to Newport News, Virginia, to pick up a shipment of new cars and deliver them to Pittsburgh. "When was the last time you saw your husband?" asked Loughran. "When his body was brought back," she replied in a soft, southern drawl as she tried to stem her tears.

Trucker Herbert Parr, a childhood friend of Pitts, happened to be driving by with a shipment of new automobiles when he saw Pitts's truck parked at 6:20 a.m. on July 28. "I recognized his truck by the copper-colored horns and braked my truck down to go over and wake him up," he told the jury. Instead, Parr found his friend lying on the front seat with his feet beneath the steering wheel.

Lester Woodward of Duncannon, Pennsylvania, died on July 25 near the Irwin Interchange, about one hundred yards from the scene of a fatal accident between four cars and two tractor trailer trucks around the approximate time of Woodward's death. Two women were killed, and seven others were injured in the fiery crash that state police initially believed was the result of a chain reaction. State police later concluded that Wable cut across the median strip from the eastbound lane into the westbound lane after killing Woodward to escape the murder scene, triggering the accident, according to the *Pittsburgh Sun-Telegraph*.

It was John Shepard's turn to testify about his meeting with Wable after Shepard testified that he thought he had suffered a stroke when a sharp pain surged through his head. The *Pittsburgh Sun-Telegraph* recounted Shepard's testimony, which mirrored an interview he had given to reporters from his hospital bed after undergoing surgery.

> *It didn't seem like I slept long when I heard something like a firecracker bursting in my right ear. I jumped up in the middle of the seat for a few minutes. I thought I was home. I don't know why, but I think I yelled twice for my mother. I couldn't see for a while. Then I realized blood was coming from my right ear. I had some paper towels in the truck. I got some of them, got out on the right side, walked to the front and saw a pair of auto headlights approaching. A man got out and spoke to me, referring to the turnpike killings.*

Loughran walked over to the defense table, where Wable was sitting. "Is this the man?" "That's him right there. I know he was a good bit taller than me. He spoke to me and made a reference to the Turnpike Killer." Shepard wasn't as positive when he first saw Wable at the state police barracks in Greensburg after Wable returned from New Mexico.

"Do you remember what he said?" Loughran asked.

> *He said something about a turnpike killer, and I said, "No, sir. Something busted in my head." The man said he would help me and told me to get in my truck and lay down. Some time passed, but he said something about he would go and get help and asked me for money because he didn't have enough for gas. He went away in the car, and he turned around in front of the truck and the truck lights shined in his car. I saw him very plainly.*

Wable told Shepard to remove his pants because "'That will cool off your blood,' he said, and said it won't flow so fast. I got my trousers down as far as my shoes, and then he helped me get over my shoes with them." Shepard's wallet was attached by a wire to his belt, along with a yellow gold

Elgin pocket watch. Loughran showed Shepard the watch. "Yes, that is my watch," Shepard replied, according to a story in the *Pittsburgh Press.*

"When I came to, I was lying on the seat," Shepard continued. "I was cold and reaching for my trousers. They weren't there. I sat up and saw a truck coming and flashed my lights. A truck pulled beside me. I can't remember the conversation, but I tried to explain that something was wrong. In the meantime, an ambulance pulled up, and I said, 'That's for me.'"

"Mr. Shepard, I want to ask you this: Was there anyone else with Wable?" asked Loughran. "I could only see one person," replied Shepherd.

The *Pittsburgh Press* recounted the testimony of Westmoreland County detective Merle Musick, who read Wable's confession to the jury. He said he and state police corporal William Smith were engaged in idle conversation on the train when Musick asked Wable about the murders.

"Smith was familiar with Farmington, Pennsylvania [Wable's home district], and they talked about it," Musick testified. "Smith left the compartment about 5:30 p.m., and I asked Wable about the Turnpike Killer. He said, 'You wouldn't believe me if I told you.'" Wable said he had been with Jim Parks and that they had gone up to Donegal on the turnpike and shot a trucker. He said, 'Jim Parks did it, but I was with him.'"

Musick testified that he then gave Wable a pencil and paper and that Wable began writing. Parks, according to Wable, drove a Cadillac and wore fashionable clothes. Wable was unable to provide other details, such as where Parks lived, but provided investigators with a vague physical description.

Corporal Smith testified that he searched for Jim Parks but had been unable to find any person who matched Wable's limited description. Smith said he scoured the Ohiopyle area of Fayette County and canvassed bars in Pittsburgh with a photograph of Wable to find out if anybody saw him with another man resembling Parks. "Many times, I made a special effort to get information from John Wesley Wable relative to Parks. He was never able to tell me where Parks lived or give me a complete description of him. He was never able to convince me that Jim Parks exists," Smith testified.

The courtroom was filled with tension. Jim Delaney, a reporter covering the trial for the *Pittsburgh Post-Gazette*, had a bad cold and couldn't stop coughing and sniffling during testimony. A testy Bauer offered some medical advice. "Whoever has that cold should take some cough syrup or codeine. That will clear it up," reported the *Uniontown Morning Herald*.

Leora Crissey, Wable's former girlfriend, was a damning witness against Wable, because she linked him to the murder weapon that he had hidden in her stepfather's house before he fled Cleveland. Crissey was a plump, blond waitress and divorced mother of a three-year-old daughter who lived with her mother, Elsie, and stepfather, John Jandura, in Bedford Heights, a few miles outside Cleveland. She wore a checked suit and white blouse as she took the witness stand, and at times, she found it difficult to answer some of Loughran's questions, chewing on her lip as she looked down at her hands folded in her lap.

When Wable returned to Cleveland after his release from the Pennsylvania jail, he went to see Crissey, who testified she saw Wable on the morning of July 28 between 10:00 and 11:00 a.m.

"Did he say he had a car?" Loughran asked.

"I don't recall," she replied.

"Did he say where he had been the night before?" Crissey said Wable didn't reveal where he had been.

She told the jury that Wable had first shown the murder weapon to her while they were sitting in his car. He kept the weapon in the glove compartment, along with a box of ammunition. Wable hid the gun in the Jandura home before he was arrested for stealing the rental car and returned to Pennsylvania, where he spent six weeks in the Fayette County Jail. After his release, he stole another car in Uniontown and drove to Cleveland to retrieve the gun. Elsie Jandura testified that Wable was "practically a member of the family. He was a nice guy. He seemed to be harmless, and he was crazy about my daughter." That account differed from what Crissey told Cleveland police and reporters after Wable's arrest. She told the *Cleveland Plain Dealer* in an interview:

> *I last saw him at a drive-in theater. He was hanging around the refreshment stand and didn't know I was there. Later that night, he telephoned my home. My mother spoke to him because I wouldn't have anything to do with him. He told me he had a new car, but I knew he hadn't been working and must have stolen it. He really started wearing on my nerves the previous Monday when he parked himself in my house at noon and didn't leave until late in the evening.*

Elsie Jandura testified that Wable warned her not to snoop in the China closet after she saw him hide something inside. 'I'm putting something in here. Don't touch it.'" Joseph Jandura was incensed when he discovered that Wable had stashed the gun in his home without telling him. The Janduras wondered aloud where Wable got his money to live on from since he had quit his job at Parker Appliance Co., but Wable mentioned that he had three job offers and was unsure of which one to accept. Then he asked John Jandura to return his gun, but when Jandura told him the police had his gun, Wable quickly changed the subject. The Janduras ordered Wable to stay away from Leora until he could porove he had a job.

Loughran called Charles Welch, twenty, to testify. Welch had shared a cell with Wable at the Fayette County Jail when Wable admitted to him that he was the Turnpike Phantom. "One evening, he asked me if I'd believe something that he told me," Welch testified. "He said he was the Turnpike Killer." Before Welch was released, he told prison officials about the conversation, and they, in turn, notified state police. Pennsylvania State Police detectives John Cherin and Frank McKetta questioned Welch about the conversation and examined the rental car that had been recovered, but by then, Wable was on his way back to Cleveland.

Wable had expressed an unusual interest in Welch's whereabouts and called the jail three times to find out when Welch would be released. Warden Jack L. Cochrane testified that he suspected Wable was planning to kill Welch, and that's why he asked about Welch's whereabouts. Fayette County district attorney Fred Brothers questioned Welch about Wable's boasts and said, "His story rings true." Wable also contacted one of Welch's sisters, Mrs. Steven Kubitsky, who testified that Wable showed up at her house one weekend looking for her brother.

Joseph Kunkle, a turnpike toll taker, testified that Wable exited the turnpike at the Irwin Interchange but didn't have any money to pay the fifteen-cent toll, so the worker paid it for him. Kunkle had seen Wable twice before, once when Kunkle was fishing at Ohiopyle and a second time at a Howard Johnson's restaurant. The night before Pitts was killed, Wable bought Kunkle a cup of coffee at the restaurant.

"Did you recognize him?" Loughran asked.

> *Yes, I did. I told him I'd seen him fishing the other day. We had quite a talk at the toll gate. He told me his brother had asked to meet him there and he was waiting for him. I invited him into the tollbooth, and we talked about two hours. He said he didn't have any money. He said he was in a restaurant and lost his pocketbook. I said, "Well, one good turn deserves another. You bought the coffee last night, and I'll pay the toll fare for you." He thanked me very kindly and left.*

Before leaving, Wable asked Kunkle, "What would happen if they caught you making a U-turn on the turnpike?" Kunkle thought it was

The lanes of the turnpike were long and smooth, with few curves making travel pleasant. *From the National Archives.*

strange question to ask, but Loughran further cemented Wable's presence on the turnpike with testimony from waitress Ruth Pinkerton, who served coffee to a very nervous Wable at the Howard Johnson's during the early morning hours on July 25, after Pitts was murdered. She knew Wable by sight because he had been frequenting the restaurant for three weeks.

Loughran finished presenting the state's case with testimony from Sergeant Edward Crowthers, a state police ballistics expert; Dr. Mary Crumlish, a pathologist; Trooper David Drenning; and Dr. Mary Willard, a chemistry professor at Penn State University. Crowthers testified that he matched the bullet removed from Pitts's brain to a test firing from the murder weapon. "What did you find?" Loughran asked. "It is my opinion that the bullet removed from the head of Harry Pitts was discharged from that gun," responded Crowthers.

Drenning told the jury that he made plaster casts of the bloody tire tracks of the stolen car Wable was believed to have been driving the night Pitts was murdered. He said the tracks indicated the car drove past Pitts's truck and pulled off the berm. Then the vehicle backed up and stopped beside the tractor trailer. The path of the vehicle indicated Wable drove past the front of the truck and crossed the highway into the opposite lane, triggering the deadly six-car accident. Dr. Willard testified that she analyzed the tire tracks and said they matched the tires on the rental car Wable was driving. Dr. Crumlish testified that the bullet passed through the frontal lobe of Pitts's brain and went through his left eye socket before becoming embedded in the left side of his jaw. "Death was instantaneous," she said. "He would only have lived a fraction of a second."

10

CONFRONTING WABLE

The prosecution rested its case after presenting its final witnesses. Now, it was Wable's turn to tell his side of the story. But his lawyers were worried because they knew Loughran would put Wable through a relentless cross-examination in an effort to dismantle his story about Jim Parks. Loughran would attempt to destroy Wable's credibility and prove to the jury that he was not an accomplice but the gunman who killed Pitts. Wable faced rapid-fire questions from the stocky prosecutor that shook Wable's demeanor, causing him to lash out at Loughran. Ethically, Scales could not allow Wable to lie under oath, but he had to persuade the jury that Parks existed in the hopes that if the jury did convict Wable of murder, he might be spared the death penalty.

Prosecutors and police believed that Parks was a figment of Wable's imagination, conjured to lessen Wable's complicity and create an alternative suspect in the case. Even if Scales personally doubted his client's story, he was ethically bound to raise the issue to try to persuade the jury that Parks existed. Scales guided Wable through a series of questions on direct examination about the events surrounding the killings and how he first met Jim Parks by chance at a Pittsburgh bus station. It was a difficult task for Scales to sell to the jury a story of a country bumpkin from Fayette County hooking up with a sophisticated counterfeiter in downtown Pittsburgh.

Scales had tried criminal and civil cases and served as a municipal solicitor in his hometown of Trafford, a small town that straddles both Westmoreland and Allegheny Counties. Testimony from the newspaper stories in Greensburg, Pittsburgh, Monessen, Uniontown and Cleveland revealed that Scales limited his questioning of Wable, since Loughran would only be able to question Wable about his answers to questions asked on a four-hour direct examination from Scales. Scales stood at one end of the jury box, arms folded, questioning his client, while Wable sat on the witness stand, his hands in his lap and his fingers intertwined as he answered Scales in a soft voice.

"Did you shoot or wound Pitts?" Scales asked.

"I did not," Wable replied.

"Did you have anything to do with this shooting?"

"I did not."

"Did you shoot or wound Woodward early in the morning of July 25 or any other time?"

"I did not."

"Did you have anything to do with that shooting?"

"I did not."

Scales then asked if Wable had shot Shepard, but Wable was evasive. "I know a little bit. I came through there that morning. There was a man who told me he was shot by the turnpike bandit. He asked me to get an ambulance. I was handling counterfeit money and didn't want to be involved with police. I let things go."

"What did you do?" Scales continued.

"He flagged me down. He had blood all over his face and eyes. I pulled in front of his truck in my car and helped him get back in the cab."

"Do you know anything else?" asked Scales

"Not in the least," said Wable.

Wable had told police a different tale while he was in custody. He said he and Parks drove to Ohio and saw Shepard's truck parked along the road. Parks left the vehicle and returned a short time later. Wable had talked to Shepard and was waiting for Parks. "Jim got in and said he didn't kill the driver and asked me what I said to him. I told him, and he gave me hell and then he told me he would fix him good. He took the car and left me standing along the road," according to the statement he gave police on the train.

When Parks returned to get Wable, he was carrying a pair of pants. "When he came back, I thought he had finished him off, but I know different now. He had a pair of pants with him. He said we would get rid of them." Then the two men drove to Lisbon, Ohio, and burned the pants in a roadside ditch. The reason for taking Shepard's pants remains a mystery. It never was explained why the pants were taken or that removing Shepard's pants would have stemmed the bleeding from his head wound. Parks gave Wable the pocket watch that Wable claimed Parks took from Shepard. Wable later pawned it in Cleveland. Parks, said Wable, asked if he wanted to continue passing counterfeit money.

"He asked me if I wanted to make some easy money, and I told didn't know what he meant. He said it was easy. I gave him some money, and he gave me double what I gave him, but it was counterfeit—in tens and twenties. I passed the money in theaters and other places. I saw Parks several times that day and met him several times later at the Fort Pitt Hotel."

"How much counterfeit money did you pass for Jim Parks?" asked Scales.

"About $4,000 or $5,000 in June and July," Wable replied.

Scales then asked Wable about Parks's physical description.

"He's about five feet, six inches tall, shorter than I am, and weighs about 140 to 150 pounds. He's red-faced and has curly, wavey hair. His cheeks are hollow. He wears sport clothes, and you seldom see him with a tie on. He has a very large diamond ring on his left hand. He's about thirty-five or forty."

Wable said he once followed Parks in a car to see where he lived but he was unsuccessful because Parks ran several red lights in the heavy Pittsburgh traffic. "I followed Parks but couldn't keep up, so I started toward home on Route 51. I was tired, stopped at a restaurant and went to sleep in my car. I must have slept until 10:00 a.m. on July 24. Then I went home. I stayed home until the evening meal with my family. Then I went to the Dinner Bell, where I danced and had something to drink and eat."

Wable told Scales that the statement he gave on the train ride from New Mexico to Greensburg was coerced from him by Detective Merle Musick, even though Wable admitted in his confession that he was treated well by the police and confessed to the crimes freely. Now, on trial for his life, Wable claimed he was threatened and physically abused by Musick in the compartment they shared.

Loughran's cross-examination of Wable was unyielding and lasted for over five hours. He attacked Wable's credibility. First, Loughran asked Wable about the statement he gave authorities in New Mexico, in which he said that he owned the murder weapon. Wable then backtracked, claiming that the statement was incorrect and that he had never read it. "I didn't read the statement. They were rushing me through so they could take me out and put me on TV," he testified. "I never read the statement. I just looked it over."

"Yet yesterday, you said the things in the statement were true." Loughran said.

Then Wable testified that the statement he gave Musick on the train was coerced.

"What did they do to you?" Loughran asked.

"Musick was roughing me up a bit, elbowing and punching me. I wrote a statement, but I was told what to write."

"Why didn't you yell for help?"

"What was the use? I couldn't be heard."

"Weren't you served your meals on the train?

"Yes, sir."

"And you never complained to them [the attendants]?"

"No, sir. The colored boys that came in were even scared to come in the door."

"Were you threatened?"

"Yes, they said if I wouldn't write it [the confession], I would get more of the same."

"You said Corporal Smith treated you like a gentleman. Did you ever complain to Mr. Smith?"

"No, sir. He would just take a walk, and I would have gotten more of the same."

Smith had testified earlier that Wable admitted to him that he was aware that Parks planned to kill Pitts. Wable told him, "I knew he was either going to rob or kill" and that Parks gave him $500 to keep quiet about the slaying.

Wable, at one point, grew angry over Loughran's rapid-fire questions that were designed to break his alibi and accused the prosecutor of lying. "You know my history from the day I was born, and you know a lot of lies," said Wable. "I know a lot about you, Johnny, and it's not a lot of lies," reported the *Pittsburgh Press.*

Loughran called Westmoreland County Jail warden William Hohn, who testified that Wable was given a physical exam after he arrived at the county jail, to counter Wable's claim that he was forced into making the statement. "After a very close check, I found the only marks on his body were scars from old acid burns on the inside surface of his right leg," Hohn testified.

"There were no other marks?" asked Loughran.

"There were not," Hohn replied.

Loughran then turned to question to Charles Welch, who was Wable's cellmate when they were lodged in the Fayette County Jail. Welch had testified earlier for the prosecution that Wable admitted to him that he was the Turnpike Killer. Welch also said that he had known Wable for about five years prior to their incarceration, but Wable said that wasn't true. "I didn't know Welch until that time in jail. But once, I think, we went Halloweening together."

"You were friends in jail?"

"That's right."

"Did you see Charley Welch in jail in Uniontown?"

"Yes," replied Wable.

"Did you tell him that you were the Turnpike Killer?"

"I did not. He was there for violating a twenty-year parole, and he only said that to the cops so he could get out. I never made no statement like that. If there had been a conversation like that, three or four other men would have heard it."

Loughran then switched to questions about Wable's encounter with Shepard.

Wable said, "I saw him bleeding on the face. He couldn't make it back into the truck, and I helped him into the truck and told him to lie down."

"Did he ask you to call an ambulance, and did you tell him you didn't have any money for gasoline?"

"He asked for help, but I didn't ask him for money. I didn't take any money. I pulled up there and talked to him."

"You want the court to believe you came along and didn't summon help?"

"I didn't call for help because I was handling counterfeit money at the time."

Wable was vague in his response to many questions and often said he couldn't remember certain details. Why then, Loughran demanded to know, could he remember explicit details about his activities on certain nights, yet couldn't answer general questions?

"Anybody charged with murder would sit down and figure out what he did on those dates," Wable replied. Wable had testified that he was a military policeman after enlisting with the army on August 14, 1948, and said he received a medical discharge on February 7, 1949. But Loughran produced documents showing that Wable was court-martialed for larceny and dishonorably discharged.

During his questioning of Wable's father, William, Loughran attempted to portray the defendant as a different person than the one described by the defense. Even though Wable may have attended church as a boy, his father conceded that he hadn't attended Sunday services for over three years. William Wable admitted that the "good boy" portrayed by his family had stolen a car and broken into a service station.

"Do you remember if he ever took money from the house?" Loughran asked.

"He took some but said it wasn't him. It was about $200," said William.

"Seems like he got blamed for a lot of things he didn't do." Loughran said.

"I guess so," replied William Wable. "I never found out who took the money, and I never got it back," William testified.

"What did you do about it?" continued Loughran.

"What can you do? He didn't get along well in the army. He said he got a medical discharge. He used to come home from Cleveland and bring guys with him."

"Did he ever bring Jim Parks home with him?" asked Loughran.

"Not that I know of."

Scales summoned two alibi witnesses to place Wable in Solon, Ohio, at the time of the Pitts murder. Eugene Weber, a seventeen-year-old gas station attendant, and rookie Solon police officer Eugene Ockunzzi remembered seeing Wable at the Sunoco gas station. Weber claimed he saw Wable in Solon at 2:30 a.m. on July 28. Pitts was murdered between 1:00 a.m. and 3:00 a.m., according to autopsy results.

"How do you remember that?" asked Scales.

"Because I'd seen him there at different times, and the second time was July 28. I remember because he told me there had been another killing on the turnpike. I read about in the newspaper, and that's how I remember the date. The first time I saw him was on the day before, about 12:30 a.m. in the morning. That was the twenty-eighth."

Ockunzzi turned out to be a better witness for the prosecution than the defense. He testified that he could not remember the exact day in July when he saw Weber and Wable together, but he told the jury that he overheard the conversation between the two men as Wable sat in his car talking to Weber.

"In the conversation that was passed from the car to the defendant was something about John Wable's ability to travel back and forth to the turnpike in record time," testified Ockunzzi.

After lunch, Weber was recalled to the witness stand and testified that he was certain he saw Wable at the station on July 28.

"Did anything call your attention to any date in the last week of July?" asked Scales.

"A newspaper article," replied Weber.

"What was that?"

Weber testified that he saw Wable the same day an article about the turnpike killings appeared in the *Cleveland Plain Dealer*. An angry Loughran lashed out at Weber on the witness stand, accusing him of lying about the time and date and accusing Scales of coaching the witness. "Are you going to let him alibi his way out of this?" Loughran yelled at Weber, according the *Cleveland Plain Dealer.*

Loughran threw one final monkey wrench into the defense's strategy by calling John Kettl, a special agent in charge of the U.S. Secret Service in Pittsburgh, to rebut Wable's claims that he was helping Parks circulate counterfeit currency. Kettl said that between June 1 and November 30, 1953, agents confiscated $1,626 in small denominations of bogus bills that was used as evidence in two criminal cases. "We received no $50 notes," Kettl said. "Was Jim Parks ever brought to your attention?" Loughran asked. "He was not," replied Kettl.

The Verdict

Both sides rested their cases, and the attorneys prepared to deliver their closing arguments. The trial had been emotionally and physically draining on the attorneys and the jurors. The prosecution presented compelling evidence linking Wable to Pitts's killing. Attorneys tend to review the evidence in their closing arguments with jurors in the best light possible, but what's important in reaching a verdict is how the jurors remember the facts. Scales delivered his closing argument first since the prosecution had the burden of proving Wable's guilt beyond a reasonable doubt.

"He doesn't look to be the type of person who would perform an atrocious crime like this. There are so many doubts, so many loopholes. We can't convict on a crime like this. We are going to have to live with ourselves," argued Scales, according to the *Uniontown Morning Herald*. Scales tried to sow doubt in the jurors' minds regarding turnpike toll taker John Kunkle, who placed Wable on the turnpike near the murder scene the night that Pitts was killed. "There probably is lingering doubt in the minds of jurors, which they will hold if they live to be 150 years old," Scales said.

Scales told the jury he believed Jim Parks was a real person but said that the man likely used an alias so he would not have to reveal his true name to Wable. The defense placed Wable's fate in the less-than-believable testimony of Eugene Weber, the young Ohio gas station attendant who placed Wable in Solon at the time Pitts was killed. According to the *Pittsburgh Press*, Scales stated:

> *If you believe the testimony of the young gas station attendant, that Wable was in Ohio in the early morning of July 28, the defendant could not have committed the crime. If Wable is guilty, we can find no motive nor reason.*

> *If someone else is guilty, we can still find no motive. The commonwealth could not find one. If you believe the evidence presented here, even Wable's statement to police* [blaming Jim Parks], *this crime is no higher than second-degree murder*
>
> *I ask you to temper justice with mercy, because the state's evidence is based on opinion and supposition. It is always better to be especially cautious rather than to err. It is rather inconsistent to me that the commonwealth asks you to take the life of this young boy when they already admitted they're still looking for Jim Parks. What a hollow victory a conviction would be for the commonwealth. Its case is full of loopholes. The ballistics expert gave circumstantial evidence based on opinion. If there was circumstantial evidence based on fact, that would be something else.*

Scales reminded the jury that Wable did stop to aid Shepard. "If he is the brutal slayer, would he have helped Shepard back into his truck?"

After Scales finished, it was the prosecution's turn. The short, broad-shouldered Loughran began his closing argument by telling the jury that even if Jim Parks existed and pulled the trigger killing Pitts, Wable was equally as guilty as if he had fired the murder weapon. "The law says that any time a person uses a deadly weapon on a vital part of a man's body, then there is intent to kill," reported the *Uniontown Morning Herald*. Loughran pointed out the critical testimony of turnpike toll taker John Kunkle, who talked with Wable shortly after state police believed Pitts was killed. "John Kunkle had no axe to grind. He's a schoolteacher merely making a living by acting part time as a toll taker."

Then, pointing at Wable, Loughran launched an attack on Wable's credibility.

> *Who is this Jim Parks? Is Jim Parks another name for John Wesley Wable? There are too many loopholes in his story. How can you believe a man like this? Thirty-three times during my five-hour cross-examination, I caught this man in inconsistencies or whatever you want to call them. We can't bring you eyewitnesses because the man who killed Harry Pitts didn't give him a chance. He was a man who shot a person who was asleep. There is no mercy for a man who kills a sleeping man. We have, in this case, the kind of man the laws of murder were made for, the kind of man the electric chair was made for. I ask you to find this man guilty of murder in the first degree and the set the penalty of death.*

Loughran almost sounded apologetic when addressing the jurors about the issue of the death penalty. He said it was a punishment that should not be taken lightly but was custom-made for a killer like Wable. "I have asked for it [the death penalty] only twice in my ten years as an assistant district attorney," said Loughran as he wiped his forehead. "But I feel I have done by duty toward Mrs. Pitts, whose husband was murdered at the age of thirty-six."

Today, before a jury can recommend the death penalty for an individual convicted of murder, a separate trial must be held. The same jury that convicted a person of murder must listen to additional testimony before rendering a verdict on their sentence. The prosecution and defense present evidence of aggravating and mitigating circumstances before reaching a decision. If the aggravating circumstances outweigh the mitigating, the jury is required to impose a death sentence. If the mitigating circumstances outweigh the aggravating, a life sentence is required. If a jury is unable to reach a unanimous decision, the judge will impose life.

Loughran expressed sympathy for Wable's parents and stopped short of accusing them of perjury after they gave their son an alibi for the night Pitts was murdered. "They're the ones that suffer in cases like this. I'm not castigating the Wable family for saying that....Here was a mother and father trying to do all they can," reported the *Greensburg Morning Review*.

For more than three hours, Judge Bauer explained the law that the jury must apply when reaching a decision on the possible verdicts. They could exonerate Wable and find him not guilty. They could find him guilty of second-degree or first-degree murder. If their verdict was murder in the first degree, the panel would have to decide whether to recommend death in the electric chair or for Wable to spend the remainder of his life in prison. Bauer said there was no evidence presented that would allow the jury to consider the lesser verdict of manslaughter. He pointed out to the jury the fact that Wable had to climb onto the running board of the truck cab of Harry Franklin Pitts to shoot him, which was proof of premeditated murder.

"The final decision rests in your hands. Do not be blind to your duty to the state and the defendant. Be not blinded to the interests of society nor by pity for this young man," advised Bauer. "You must follow the path of evidence and turn neither to the left or right. If through fear, pity, indignation, you allow your minds to wander, you err."

Bauer then interjected a prejudicial comment that surprisingly was not raised on appeal by his defense team. "It is my opinion that the verdict can be none other than murder in the first degree." The jury is the sole determiner of that fact, so Bauer's comment was extraordinary and may have influenced the jury's decision to impose the death penalty.

The panel began deliberating at 12:18 p.m. and returned a verdict at 4:02 p.m. Defense attorney B. Patrick Costello had just gone to get a haircut in a barbershop located behind the courthouse when he received a phone call to return immediately to Bauer's courtroom. "My client's going to get the death penalty," he said. "They came back too soon," reported the *Greensburg Morning Review*.

Wable was led into the hushed courtroom as forty spectators took their seats. His family sat stoically, waiting for the jurors to enter the jury box. Court clerk Betty Flanigan asked forewoman Betty Marmie if the jury had reached a verdict.

"Prisoner, look upon the jurors," Flanigan ordered. "Jurors, look upon the prisoner."

Marmie announced the verdict. "Guilty…first-degree murder…death penalty." A woman in the crowd gasped aloud, "Oh, the poor boy." Scales asked the judge to poll the jury, and each member repeated the verdict and sentence, according to the *Pittsburgh Post-Gazette*.

Wable's lips twitched as the decision was announced. His mother and two sisters began sobbing uncontrollably. His brother, Robert, faced a courtroom wall and began weeping. "I don't understand how they could bring in this verdict. I didn't do anything," Wable told Scales after the sentence was announced. Scales complained to reporters that the defense was faced with defending Wable for three separate crimes, even though he was only charged with killing Pitts. The introduction of evidence from the Woodward murder and the wounding of Shepard made it difficult to defend Wable. "We had three cases to defend instead of one," Scales told reporters after the verdict was announced.

One juror told reporters after the trial ended that there was never any doubt that Wable was guilty as soon as they walked into the jury room to deliberate. The question remained whether to send him to his death or to allow him to spend the rest of his life in prison. The jury voted eight times and were split seven to five over the sentence. On the ninth ballot, they unanimously agreed to the death penalty. Another juror said they believed Wable and Parks "were one in the same man."

The first stage of the appeals process begins before the county court. Wable appealed to a panel of three judges that included Bauer, Richard Laird and John O'Connell, who rejected his arguments for a new trial. They wrote that the "testimony admitted at the trial relative to other crimes is linked with events and facts necessary to prosecute the matter at issue." The next step is to appeal to the Pennsylvania Supreme Court, but Wable had to be formally sentenced.

Wable returned to court on December 28 to face Judge Bauer. He was ordered to stand while Scales, Costello and McCormick stood around him. The impact of Bauer's words filled the quiet courtroom. "The sentence of the law is that you suffer death during the week fixed by the governor of the commonwealth. May God, in his infinite goodness, have mercy on your soul," intoned Bauer. The phrase "may God…have mercy on your soul" dates to biblical times, when rabbinical courts in Israel read the phrase as a prayer for the condemned.

Bauer asked Scales if he had anything to say. "There's not much more to be said at this time. The jury has spoken."

Before Wable was sentenced, Bauer asked him if he had anything to say before his sentence was pronounced. Wable replied:

> *I was convicted by the newspapers before the trial, and I am not guilty. The district attorney asked me if I would take a lie detector test, and I said I would. But then he wouldn't let me. I am not guilty of this crime I am going to be sentenced for. I told the state cops I would take them to Pittsburgh and show them where he* [Parks] *was at and get him for them. They said they would take me in, but they refused, and they never did.*

As Wable was led from the courtroom by deputies, he smiled and winked at his family. He would remain in the Westmoreland County Jail until the day of his scheduled execution and then be delivered to the state penitentiary at Rockview in Centre County, where executions in the electric chair were carried out until 1962. In the meantime, his defense team prepared an appeal to the Pennsylvania Supreme Court. Warden William Hohn said Wable had few visitors in the weeks following the verdict. "He's been pretty well left alone. His mother came to see him once since the conviction, but his father has never been here. His brother, Robert, comes in once in a while."

Wable spent his days reading comic books and waiting for a decision on his appeal from the Pennsylvania Supreme Court. It came late in the day on May 23, 1955. The main argument posited by the defense attorneys was that Judge Bauer erred in letting evidence from the Woodward murder and Shepard shooting into the trial of Wable for the Pitts killing. They also argued that Wable's attorneys were not given the opportunity to examine the murder weapon or the reports of the two psychiatrists who examined Wable on behalf of the prosecution.

The justices found little merit in their arguments. Chief Justice Horace Stern wrote that while, normally, the introduction of evidence from other crimes is not allowed, there are exceptions when "there is such a logical connection between the crimes that proof of one will naturally tend to show the accused is the person who committed the other.

"A careful reading of the testimony leads to the conclusion that the jury was well justified in finding that defendant was the person who committed these outrageous, deliberate and brutal crimes," Stern wrote in *Commonwealth v. Wable*.

As to the psychiatric reports, Stern said the defense also had a psychiatrist examine Wable, but the attorneys never raised the insanity defense at the trial. The justices also wrote that Loughran's mention that alibi witness Eugene Weber had been coached on what to say was not prejudicial. "The district attorney, however, merely stated what was a fact, nor did it carry any such necessary implication. The trial was fair, impartial and conducted by the court painstakingly and in meticulous regard for all of the defendant's legal rights," read the court's opinion.

Warden Hohn didn't tell Wable the bad news until the next day. "He took it very calmly and told me he still has hopes that he'll get a reprieve," Hohn said.

11

A PICTURE IS WORTH A THOUSAND WORDS

When Wable returned to the Westmoreland County Courthouse three days after Christmas in 1954 to be formally sentenced to death in the electric chair, newspapers chafed at the judicial edict that prevented their photographers from taking pictures of the convicted killer anywhere inside the courthouse. News photographers were still banned from photographing Wable on his way to or from the courtroom or of Sheriff Howard "Bud" Thomas, his deputies or any witnesses. Bauer said he issued his ruling to protect the privacy of the defendant. "A defendant is entitled to a fair trial before a jury and not to be hindered by some outside influence," Bauer told the *Pittsburgh Post-Gazette*. "When a man is being tried for a serious crime, his picture is not to be put in the paper. It might affect the trial."

The Wable trial wasn't the first sensational murder case to rock the serenity of small-town Greensburg and attract hordes of publicity. In 1947, Dominick Daverse stalked his ex-wife, Theresa, as she rode a bus from her job in South Greensburg and disembarked in front of the courthouse.

Prosecuting and defense attorneys have always been concerned about extensive pretrial publicity of a sensational case because it can make it difficult for them to pick an unbiased jury. Usually, there is a gap between the time a defendant is arrested and when the case goes to trial, but in Wable's case, his trial began in March 1954 after his October 1953 arrest. A verdict in another highly publicized murder trial that year was overturned by the U.S. Supreme Court because of overwhelming news coverage. Dr.

The interior of the Westmoreland County Courthouse in Greensburg, where Wable was convicted of murder and sentenced to death. *Courtesy of Westmoreland County.*

Sam Sheppard, an Ohio neurosurgeon, had his conviction for killing his wife overturned when the justices ruled that the trial judge had failed to protect Sheppard's right to due process.

Photographers snapped a photograph of Judge Bauer on his way to the courthouse one morning, prompting Bauer to ban the photographers from standing on the courthouse steps. In an act of defiance, photographers posed on the courthouse steps, their cameras sitting at their feet, for a picture that was published in Pittsburgh newspapers. Bauer's ban didn't stop them from taking photographs of the jury taking a stroll on a public street during a lunch break or of Wable's family, the defense attorneys or Wable's former girlfriend, Leora Crissey, eating lunch in a Greensburg restaurant.

The Wable trial attracted reporters from the *Pittsburgh Sun-Telegraph*, *Pittsburgh Press*, *Pittsburgh Post-Gazette*, *Greensburg Morning Review*, *Greensburg Daily Tribune*, *Uniontown Morning and Evening Standard* and *Cleveland Plain Dealer*, along with wire service reporters from the Associated Press and United Press International. Between twenty and thirty photographers descended on the courthouse on the trial's opening day, hoping to photograph Wable. The news coverage was extensive across Pennsylvania, as well as across the country. Stories on Wable's crimes, arrest, trial, conviction and pending execution were carried by the *New York Times* and *Washington Post*, as well as newspapers in Ohio, New Mexico, Indiana, Texas, North Carolina, Florida, Iowa, Connecticut, Maryland, Montana and Kansas.

Lawyers for the Greensburg newspapers and *Pittsburgh Post-Gazette* appealed to a federal judge in Pittsburgh to lift the ban. "The press regards this case as a fundamental right of the freedom of the press," argued attorney Fred Trescher, who represented the Tribune-Review Publishing Co. at a hearing to lift the ban before U.S. District Judge Wallace Gourley. The company published the *Greensburg Morning Review*, founded in 1886, and the *Greensburg Daily Tribune*, which began publishing in 1902. The two papers merged in 1955. Trescher argued that "newsworthiness is a fleeting thing."

> *It is important that we put pictures of a principal individual in the publication on the day he makes news, not the next month, not the next day or a week or a month later. A person loses that right to privacy when he gets into a public proceeding, and the public has a right to be informed what is happening in a public trial.*

Attorney Paul McCormick, whose son Richard was one of Wable's defense attorneys, represented the county in federal court. He argued newspapers "have confused freedom of the press with picture taking. The county court order has not denied the right of publishing news about the trial. You can publish pictures of people in the trial. However, the court has merely said that at certain times, at certain places, you cannot take pictures. There are limitations only of time and place."

Bauer banned photographers from taking any pictures of the defendant in the courthouse hallways or corridors or of any jurors, attorneys or witnesses within forty feet of his courtroom door without their written permission. When Judge Gourley questioned Westmoreland County solicitor H. Reginald Belden about the scope of Bauer's ban, Belden refused to explain, telling Gourley that Bauer "declined to give an interpretation in advance." McCormick argued that the federal court was not the proper venue to appeal Bauer's ban. He said the newspapers should file an appeal in the Pennsylvania appellate courts first before seeking a federal remedy. "They know what they intend to do, and it's grossly unfair for them not to tell me what they intend to do," said Gourley, who compared Bauer's actions to tactics used by Nazis, fascists and communists to stifle free speech.

Gourley decried "the growing practice of secrecy in government and the belief among public officials that they are not accountable to the public" and that they "can conduct business of their offices in secret," reported the *Pittsburgh Post-Gazette*. "The ruling [by Judge Bauer] is too wide. It would apply to any case, anything, for all time." Gourley issued an injunction, preventing the county from enforcing the ban, and ruled photographers could take pictures anywhere in the courthouse, except in the courtroom or in the hallway and corridors leading to Bauer's courtroom.

The newspapers asked the Pennsylvania Supreme Court to review the case, but the justices said that they could not rule whether the newspapers'

First Amendment rights had been violated, since no publication had intentionally defied the order. So, Greensburg publisher David Mack and *Pittsburgh Post-Gazette* publisher William Block resolved to covertly photograph the convicted killer in the courthouse when he was brought to the courtroom for sentencing, knowing their action likely would result in charges for criminal contempt of court, which carried a penalty of jail time and fines.

Photojournalism didn't exist until 1919, when the *New York Illustrated News* published the first picture in a newspaper. Until then, publications used drawings and illustrations to document a story. By the 1920s, camera technology had become more sophisticated, and the publication of photographs became more common. Photographs of crime scenes, criminals and notable individuals began appearing more frequently in papers.

Newspapers were still the public's main source of news in the early 1950s and provided gavel-to-gavel coverage of the Wable trial. The Associated Press and United Press International rewrote local stories for statewide and national distribution. Television was in its infancy in western Pennsylvania, and radio stations used local news reports for their broadcasts. WDTV was the first television station in Pittsburgh and was in the process of changing its call letters to KDKA at the time, but the station provided little news coverage, except for a program titled "Pitt Parade," which was a compilation of news events recorded on film, according to *Broadcasting the Local News: The Early Years of Pittsburgh's KDKA TV.*

To test the ban, the publishers of the Greensburg papers and the *Pittsburgh Post-Gazette* planned a photographic ambush that was designed in such a way that no one in the immediate area would even know any pictures had been taken. *Pittsburgh Post-Gazette* reporter Vince Johnson; photographers James Klingensmith and Robert Purdy of the *Pittsburgh Post-Gazette*; and freelancer Don Bindyke, hired by the Greensburg papers, scouted the route from the jail to the courthouse and the courtroom. The county jail in the 1950s was located directly behind the courthouse so sheriff's deputies could quickly walk a prisoner from the jail to the courthouse.

Klingensmith was a veteran photographer who later became known for his iconic picture of Pittsburgh Pirate Bill Mazeroski circling the bases after hitting the game-winning ninth-inning homerun to win the 1960 World Series against the New York Yankees. He acted as the decoy. The courthouse is an elaborate building, with each floor circling an elaborately decorated rotunda trimmed with gold leaf. There were courtrooms on each floor and winding steps leading to the second floor.

A scout on the first floor lifted his hat to signal Johnson that Wable was on his way; then Johnson signaled the photographers. Klingensmith carried his bulky Speed Graphic camera in a shopping bag to draw the attention of the deputies who patrolled outside Bauer's courtroom. Speed Graphics were used in the 1950s to cover news events but were large, bulky and required flashbulbs to shoot indoors. The camera had a slow lens speed, and each picture required the operator to insert a sheet film holder into the camera. Then the lens shutter had to be opened, and the focal plane had to be cocked and focused. Purdy and Bindyke were carrying smaller, easily concealed .35-millimeter cameras containing infrared film that didn't require a flash attachment.

As deputies led Wable to the courtroom, Klingensmith pulled his camera from the bag as if to shoot when he was blocked by deputies. Meanwhile, Purdy and Bindyke snapped away, capturing Wable entering and leaving the courtroom. One picture shows a profile of Wable entering the courtroom and a second shows Wable as he is escorted down a stairway, surrounded by deputies, after the sentencing. The pictures are slightly out of focus, but Wable can clearly be seen.

The *Greensburg Daily Tribune* published the photograph and story in its afternoon edition. Westmoreland County sheriff Thomas delivered a copy to Judge Bauer as soon as the paper hit the streets. Bauer seemed unconcerned by the violation of his order when *Pittsburgh Post-Gazette* reporter Vince Johnson asked him for a comment. "I have a lot of work on my desk right now, and I'm too busy to talk about it," Bauer said. "It is really not too important."

But Bauer did act. He cited Mack, Block, Johnson, the photographers and *Post-Gazette* editor Andrew Bernhard for contempt of court for violating Judicial Canon 35, which said taking photographs detracts from the dignity of the proceedings and "degrades the court." At a hearing on the contempt charges before Judges Bauer, Richard Laird and John O'Connell, none of the witnesses who testified were aware any pictures had been taken. Sheriff Thomas said he didn't learn of the violation until he saw the pictures in the afternoon edition of the *Daily Tribune*.

"Did you notice any unusual commotion or disturbance of any sort?" Deputy Sheriff Brandon Leasure was asked.

"Oh, no. I didn't see any disturbance," he replied.

"Did you notice any commotion of any kind there?"

"No…there was a lot of people gathered around the rotunda to watch him going down; they wanted to see the prisoner. That's natural."

"No disturbance of any kind?"

"I don't see any."

David Mack, the publisher of Greensburg's two newspapers, said photographs are an integral part of telling a story.

> *A newspaper's job is to publish things of public interest in as clear a way as possible. Pictures are an important tool of the newspaper in reporting completely and accurately. The photo ban, we feel, blocks us from a public building that belongs to the people of this county and prevents us from reporting items that they have a right to know. The only possible way to resolve the situation was to violate the court order. The picture taking was not done thoughtlessly but thoughtfully so that the photo ban can be tested as we felt it should be.*

Block, publisher of the *Pittsburgh Post-Gazette*, argued at a hearing that the courthouse belongs "to the people of that county and not to the judges." He added that Bauer's order "seriously infringes on the constitutional guarantee of a free press and the people's right to know."

The *Pittsburgh Post-Gazette*'s Vince Johnson testified at the contempt hearing that the trial had national interest, as well as local attention. "The reason it [the Wable case] was covered so extensively is the case aroused national interest; on top of that, the issue as to whether or not the correct man had been apprehended was certainly important."

The judges asked the photographers why they hadn't asked Wable for his permission to have his photograph taken, as Bauer's order required. "Did you have permission of John Wesley Wable to take his picture?" O'Connell asked. "You made no attempt before his picture was taken to get permission from John Wesley Wable to photograph him?" asked Bauer. "It would have been impossible, because he was moving too fast," replied Purdy. Charles Kenworthy, another attorney representing the newspapers, said Wable was guarded by three deputies and that the photographers would not have been allowed to approach him.

Besides, Kenworthy added, judges lack the authority to regulate access to any place in the courthouse other than their courtrooms. "By what right does the court have to regulate that part of the courthouse not regulated by the courts? Freedom of the press is one of the most precious rights in this country. It means the right to publish facts. Why regulate the right to take pictures quickly without disturbing a courtroom?"

Paul McCormick argued that freedom of the press doesn't apply to cameras. The First Amendment guarantees the right of expression, not freedom to gather news wherever reporters want. He said the fact that the newspapers conspired to violate the order proved they acted "in a willfully defiant and contemptuous manner," making them guilty of contempt. The judges found the journalists guilty. Mack, Block and Bernhard were each fined $500 and sentenced to five days in jail. Johnson, Klingensmith, Purdy and Bindyke were fined $100 each and were also sentenced to five days in jail.

The convictions were appealed to the Pennsylvania Supreme Court in July 1954. Kenworthy told the justices that the defendants were "wholly innocent, and no amount of strained semantics can distort appellants' acts of taking photographs into 'conduct obstructing the administration of justice.'" He also told the justices that Westmoreland County judges had "a personal distaste for publicity."

Without referring to it directly, the Greensburg newspapers and *Pittsburgh Post-Gazette* had published stories about the corrupt political ring operating in the Westmoreland County Courthouse. The articles focused on Bauer, Laird and O'Connell and their lenient treatment of organized crime figures in the county. Bauer and Laird, along with District Attorney Alexander Sculco, were targets of Operation Crusade, a group of four hundred ministers who wanted to rid the county of vice and political corruption by opposing their reelections.

The Supreme Court upheld the contempt charges, ruling that newspapers and journalists have "no special right or privilege" that the public doesn't have. Taking photographs in the courtroom "is repugnant to the high standards of judicial decorum to which our courts are accustomed" and could open a "wedge to a gradual deteriorating of the judicial process."

Justice Michael Musmanno dissented, writing that the dignity of the court was not tarnished because the court was not in session when the pictures of Wable were taken. The cameras used by the photographers were silent and unobtrusive, he noted, and he called his colleagues' decision a "stinging blow against freedom of the press. I dissent to the ultimate."

The *Pittsburgh Post-Gazette* noted that Musmanno pointed out to his fellow justices that the publications, by violating the ban, did what the high court had suggested. The court said it could not decide if the newspapers, First Amendment rights were violated until someone challenged the ban by breaking it. "Isn't it an incongruity to impose a jail sentence on these defendants who simply did as the Supreme Court of Pennsylvania directed?"

Musmanno later said in an interview that when he served as a trial judge at the Nuremberg War Crimes Tribunal in Germany following

World War II, still photographs and moving pictures were allowed. "Not once was I aware of the taking of pictures…which were taken without interruption in the slightest. The orderly procedure…also enlightened the world," according to the *Pittsburgh Press*.

The Tribune-Review Publishing Co. and the P.G. Publishing Co. appealed Bauer's order to the U.S. Court of Appeals for the Third Circuit, asking for a review, but the judges turned down a request to hear arguments. The Pennsylvania Newspaper Publishers Association presented a petition to the U.S. Supreme Court, which refused to take the case.

In 1957, Warren County judge Alexander Flick broke precedent by permitting a photographer to take a photograph in his courtroom of Norman Moon as he was sentenced to death for the murder of Judge Allison Wade. Moon became angry after Wade ordered him to pay child support. Moon pulled out a gun and shot Wade as he sat on the bench during a court session on January 13, 1954. Flick explained his decision, saying, "Court proceedings are open to the public, and the public should be informed as to what goes on. If photographers cause no disturbance by their presence, I think they should be allowed to take pictures." Donald Bindyke, who was found in contempt in the Wable case, took the photograph of Moon being sentenced. Moon's death sentence was later commuted to life in prison.

Newspapers argued unsuccessfully in 1986 to ease the ban on taking pictures in the Westmoreland County Courthouse after a newspaper photographer took a picture of a robbery suspect in the hallway linking the courthouse annex to the courthouse. The defendant was twenty-five yards away from a courtroom, and a judge ordered deputies to confiscate the film and asked his fellow judges to review the issue. The ban remains in effect. The Westmoreland County Rules of Criminal Procedure bars photographs "of any type anywhere in the courthouse for any criminal proceeding." Even police officers must turn off body cameras before entering a courtroom.

12

"GREAT GOD, HE'S ALIVE"

Pennsylvania legislator A.B. Hess introduced legislation in Harrisburg in 1913 that replaced hanging with electrocution as the legal method of execution in the state. The condemned no longer had to climb the steps of the gallows, trussed up with restraints, and then be slowly strangled to death if the drop didn't immediately break their neck. "I'm glad condemned men could be put to death without such torture as heretofore," Hess told the *Pittsburgh Post* after his bill became law. Instead, the condemned would be strapped into a chair with thick leather belts. Then thousands of volts of electricity would surge through their brains, rendering them unconscious.

John Wesley Wable waited in the Westmoreland County Jail for a day in September 1955 when he would be driven under guard to the state prison at Rockview in Centre County, where executions were conducted. If Wable had been sentenced to death before 1913, he would have been hanged at the county jail on a wooden scaffold, and with any luck, he would have died instantly of a broken neck from the drop.

Hangings were sometimes messy affairs if the procedure wasn't done properly. The prisoner's height was measured and their weight recorded so that the hangman could calculate the length of the rope needed. The calculations had to be precise so that when a body dropped through the trapdoor, the individual's neck would break immediately. The knot of the rope had to be positioned behind their left ear. The goal was to get the body to drop through the trapdoor on the gallows quickly enough to produce between 1,000 and 1,250 pounds of torque to break the neck and sever the spinal column. The prisoner would experience a loss of consciousness as his blood pressure dropped to zero, according to the Death Penalty Information Center. If the calculations were wrong, the individual slowly strangled to death or was decapitated.

Hangmen did not always get the procedure right. The same year the Pennsylvania bill was enacted, John "Buffalo" Harris was executed in a bungled hanging in Uniontown in Fayette County, Pennsylvania. Harris calmly walked the ten steps from his cell door to the scaffold, and two deputies placed the rope around his neck, but the drop wasn't precisely calculated, causing Harris's body to drop to the ground, landing him in a squatting position beneath the scaffold, according to an account in the *Daily News Standard* in Uniontown. The deputies hoisted the rope and held it for nineteen minutes as Harris slowly strangled to death. "An instant later, the death throes had set in. The body swayed spasmodically at the end of a rope in the struggle for life. The arms were bound, and the brain was unconscious, but the physical being was fighting. Slower and slower became the convulsive movement, and then they ceased altogether," the newspaper reported.

Experts said electricity would end the gruesome method of hanging. Charles Francis Brush was an inventor who founded the Brush Electric Company in Cleveland. He encouraged the public to tour his facility, and visitors were allowed to experience the sensation of electricity coursing through their hands by simply touching the railings surrounding the dynamo. "You could feel the surge from the generator to the railing," wrote Mike Winchell in his book *The Electric War: Edison, Tesla, Westinghouse and the Race to Light the World*. "It was a harmless tickling sensation along the skin, one that elicited laughter and smiles in those who experimented with the little game."

After a bout of drinking on August 7, 1881, George L. Smith, an alcoholic dockworker, became an unwitting test subject in the first use of an electric current to kill a human being. Smith entered the Brush Electric plant and placed his arms around the generator, which killed him instantly. His body was found the next day, hands still frozen to the device. "His body went stiff upon contact—his hug giving way to a statuesque pose of an incredible and upright and well-postured man. The attendants saw Smith's body stiff as a board and quietly rushed to his aid," wrote Winchell. "They tried to pry the body away from the generator but found his hands firmly stuck to the machine, as if a magnetic force had taken hold."

Thomas Edison. *Courtesy of the Library of Congress.*

George Westinghouse. *Courtesy of the Library of Congress.*

Smith appeared to have died instantly, painlessly and without any burns or tissue damage to his body, giving Alfred P. Southwick, a dentist and inventor, an idea. Why not use electricity to execute inmates rather than hanging them, which sometimes left the condemned dangling for minutes while choking to death in what newspapers dubbed the "dance of death"? Southwick began experimenting by killing stray dogs, cats and horses using an electric current.

Uses for electricity were growing. By the nineteenth century, Thomas Edison had invented the electric lightbulb. Alessandro Volta had developed the first battery. As knowledge about electricity grew, motors, generators and electromagnets were built for use in industry. Hospitals began using electricity to treat ailments such as cancer and mental illnesses. Electricity was also utilized to power telephone and telegraph lines.

Two of America's greatest inventors, Thomas Edison and George Westinghouse, were vying for contracts to illuminate America's cities by using different methods of electrical generation. Edison developed the direct current, which produces a solid stream of electrical charge over a short distance, in contrast to Westinghouse's more powerful alternating current, which travels farther, making it a more powerful source of energy to light cities, businesses and homes. The inventors were in a marketing battle for dominance in the electrical field. Edison brought illumination to the commercial and financial districts of New York City in 1882.

In 1886, Westinghouse did the same for the city of Buffalo, but his current functioned better than Edison's because it carried the charge over a greater distance. To thwart the growing use of the alternating current, Edison persuaded New York to adopt the Westinghouse method to power the electric chair, to the dismay of Westinghouse. Edison, who helped Southwick develop the electric chair, had hoped that public disgust over the use of Westinghouse's invention would ensure that state and municipal officials would turn to his direct current method.

Southwick served on a New York state commission that researched methods of execution to determine the most humane way to dispatch a convicted killer. The committee examined gruesome methods, such as beheading, strangulation, disembowelment, drowning, poisoning and boiling or burning a person alive. It recommended, not surprisingly, the use of an alternating current to power the electric chair. "Death, as a result, is instantaneous upon its application," concluded the 1888 Report of the Commission to Investigate and Report the Most Humane and Practical Method of Carrying Into Effect the Sentence of Death in Capital Cases. "The velocity of the electric current is so great that the brain is paralyzed, is indeed dead before the nerves can communicate any sense of shock."

Edison experimented with electricity as a mean of killing a human by filming the death by electrocution of a bad-tempered circus elephant, Topsy, who had killed three handlers in three months. Topsy was led onto a pad electrified with six thousand volts as part of the test. When the charge surged through the elephant, Topsy toppled over. Edison also demonstrated the lethality of an alternating current by rigging a piece of tin beneath a metal pan of water attached to an electrode and enticed a dog to drink the water. As soon as the dog touched the metal, the animal fell dead. He also demonstrated by wiring electrodes to horses and calves to show that an alternating current could kill a man "in the ten-thousandth of a second," according to *Smithsonian* magazine.

William Kemmler became the nation's first guinea pig to die in the electric chair. He was convicted of killing his common-law wife and sentenced to death in New York's electric chair at the Auburn Prison in 1890. Westinghouse wanted his alternating current to play no role in executing Kemmler. Harold Brown, an associate of Edison and an advocate of the direct current, campaigned to brand the alternating current as the "executioner's current," according to *Edison*, Edmund Morris's 2019 biography of Thomas Edison.

Westinghouse hoped to avoid using an alternating current to kill Kemmler, so he paid for the attorneys handling Kemmler's appeal, hoping the New York appellate court would find the execution process a form of cruel and unusual punishment outlawed by the U.S. Constitution. He hired attorney William Bourke Cockran, an Irish-born lawyer who was elected to the U.S. House of Representatives. Cockran argued that unless Kemmler died immediately, the process amounts to torture.

"The act is unconstitutional because, upon its face, it provides for the infliction of an unusual penalty," reported the *New York Times*. The appellate

Left: Topsy the circus elephant was a test subject used by Thomas Edison to show death by electrocution. Topsy had killed three handlers. *From Wikipedia.*

Right: A sketch of William Kemmler. *From Wikipedia.*

court ruled that although the electrocution process was new, it was not cruel "in the sense that some certainly prolonged or tortuous procedure would be understood to be." The jurists said they had no way of determining if electrocution was a barbarous form of punishment because no one had ever been executed by electricity.

Edison was called by Cockran as a witness at a hearing on Kemmler's appeal, hoping to prove that there was no scientific basis to show that death by electrocution was swift and painless. Edison admitted he knew nothing about human anatomy or if a person felt pain while being jolted by electricity. He was also unable to say conclusively whether blood or body tissue was a better conductor of electrical current, according to Morris's biography. "Do you know anything about the conductivity of the brain?" Edison was asked. "No sir," he replied.

Edison had a theory that electrocution would be more effective if the condemned's hands were dipped in potash and their feet placed in slippers saturated in potash, according to an 1889 article titled "The New Instrument of Execution" that Harold Brown penned for the *North American Review*. Potash is potassium-laced salt that serves as an electrical conductor when it is dissolved in water. Brown claimed that potash hastens the current, leading to a quick, painless death. "There is no struggle and

A diagram of an early electric chair. *Courtesy of the Library of Congress.*

no sound," Brown wrote. "The majesty of the law has been vindicated, but no physical pain has been caused."

Despite the lack of scientific knowledge about electrocution, the New York Supreme Court upheld the lower court's decision that electrocution was a legally acceptable form of punishment:

> *We have examined this testimony and can find but little in it to warrant the belief that this new mode of execution is cruel, within the meaning of the Constitution, though it is certainly unusual. On the contrary, we agree with the court below that it removes every reasonable doubt that the application of electricity to the vital parts of the human body, under such conditions, and in the manner contemplated by the statute, must result in instantaneous and consequently in painless death.*

Kemmler was readied for his death by guards who issued him new clothes to wear and shaved the back of his head so an electrode could be placed on his skull. His shirt was cut in the back so an electrode could be attached to the lower part of his back. Two dozen incandescent lightbulbs sat on a box in the death chair to indicate if the chair was working, according to the *New York Evening World*. The *New York Times* described Kemmler's final historic moments as Warden Charles Durston ushered him into the death chamber. Standing nearby were four physicians, Carlos MacDonald, E.C. Spitzka, William T. Jenkins and C.M. Daniels. The *New York Times* described Kemmler's last moments in a gruesome account of his death.

> *"Gentlemen," Durston said, this is William Kemmler. And Kemmler bowed. "Gentlemen,"* [Kemmler] *said, "I wish you all good luck. I believe I am going to a good place, and I am ready to go. I want only to say that a great deal has been said about me that is untrue. I am bad enough. It is cruel to make me out worse." As he finished this little speech, he bowed again and was about to sit down in a chair which had been placed beside the death chair. Warden Durston, seeing this, stepped forward, and Kemmler, noticing his action, saw that the time had come, and instead of sitting where he had intended, turned and easily dropped into the seat. Still, he did it much as one might after a long walk fall into the welcome arms of an easy chair. He sat with the light from the window streaming full on his face, and immediately in front of him was the semicircle of witnesses. Warden Durston stepped to the chair, and at his request, Kemmler arose. It was desired to see whether his clothing had been so cut away at the base of the spine as to allow of a clean contact between the electrode and the flesh. It was found that the outer garments had been cut, but the lower clothing had not been so. Durston took out a pocketknife and cut two small triangular pieces out of the shirt. Then Kemmler easily settled back into the chair again. As he did so, Durston started to get the rear piece in position. A murmur of surprise passed among the witnesses when Kemmler turned calmly to the Warden and, in such tones as one might speak to a barber who was shaving him, said calmly: "Now, take your time and do it all right, warden. There is no rush. I don't want to take any chances on this thing, you know." "All right, William," answered Durston, and then* [he] *began to adjust the headpiece. Leather straps held Kemmler's forehead and chin in place, but he asked Durston to tighten the straps even more. Then he strapped Kemmler's arms and legs to the chair with eleven belts as the condemned man strained to ensure they were tight. The warden said goodbye to Kemmler as the executioner prepared to flip the switch. The great experiment of electrical*

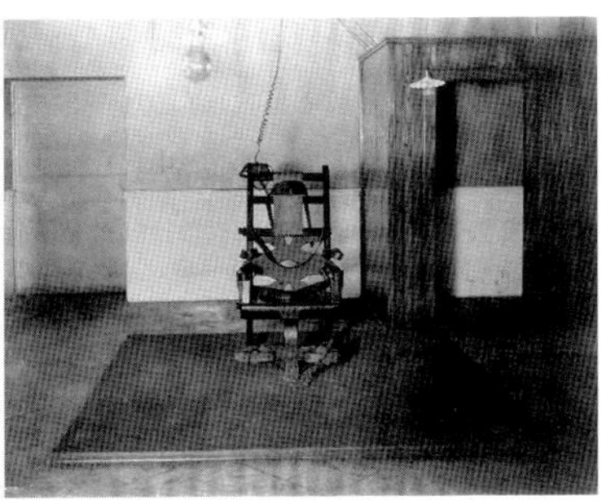

The electric chair at Auburn State Prison, where William Kemmler became the chair's first victim. *Courtesy of the Cayuga Museum.*

execution had been launched. New York State had thrown off forever the barbarities, the inhumanities of hanging its criminals. But had it? Words will not keep pace with what followed. Simultaneously with the click of the lever, the body of the man in the chair straightened. Every muscle of it seemed to be drawn to its highest tension. It seemed as though it might have been thrown across the chamber were it not for the straps which held it. There was no movement of the eyes. The body was as rigid, as though cast in bronze, save for the index finger of the right hand, which closed up so tightly that the nail penetrated the flesh on the first joint, and the blood trickled out on the arm of the chair. Drs. Spitzka and Macdonald stood in front of the chair, closely watching the dead or dying man. Beside them was Dr. Daniels, holding a stopwatch. After the first convulsion, there was not the slightest movement of Kemmler's body. An ashen pallor had overspread his features. What physicians know as the "death spots" appeared on his skin. Five seconds passed, ten seconds, fifteen seconds, sixteen and seventeen. It was just 6:43 o'clock. Dr. Spitzka, shaking his head, said: "He is dead." Warden Durston pressed the signal button, and at once, the dynamo was stopped.

However, Kemmler wasn't dead.

"Great God! He is alive!" someone said: "Turn on the current," said another. "See, he breathes," said a third. "For God's sake, kill him and have it over," said a representative of one of the press associations, and then, unable to bear the strain, he fell on the floor in a dead faint. District Attorney Quimby groaned audibly and rushed from the room. Warden Durston, who had started to loosen the electrode on the head, raised it slightly and then hastily screwed it back into place. Kemmler's body had become limp and settled down in the chair. His chest was raising and falling, and there was a heavy breathing that was perceptible to all. Kemmler was, of course, entirely unconscious. Drs. Spitzka and Macdonald kept their wits about them. Hastily, they examined the man, not touching him, however. Turning to Warden Durston, who had just finished getting the head electrode back in place, Dr. Spitzka said: "Have the current turned on again, quick—no delay." Durston sprang to the door and, in an instant, had sounded the two bells, which informed the man at the lever that the current must be turned on. Again came that click as before, and again, the body of the unconscious wretch in the chair became as rigid as one of bronze. It was awful, and the witnesses were so horrified by the ghastly sight that they could not take their eyes off it. The dynamo did not seem to run smoothly. The current could be heard sharply snapping. Blood began to appear on the face of the wretch

> *in the chair. It stood on the face like sweat. The capillary or small blood vessels under the skin were being ruptured. But there was worse than that. An awful odor began to permeate the death chamber, and then, as though to cap the climax of this fearful sight, it was seen that the hair under and around the electrode on the head and the flesh under and around the electrode at the base of the spine was singeing. The stench was unbearable. How long this second execution lasted—for it was a second execution, if there was any real life in the body when the current was turned on for the second time—is not really known by anybody. Those who held watches were too much horrified to follow them. Some said afterward that it lasted a minute. One said it lasted fully four minutes and a half. Opinions ranged all the way between those figures. Dr. Spitzka, who was as cool as any man could be under such circumstances, says it was not more than a minute. It was 6:51 o'clock when the signal went to the man at the lever to shut off the current. Kemmler had been in the chair just eight minutes from the time the current was first turned on. There is nobody among the witnesses present who can tell just how much of that time the current was passing through the body of Kemmler. As soon as the current was off again, Warden Durston rapidly unscrewed the electrodes and unbuckled the straps. Kemmler's body again was limp. This time, he was surely dead. There was no doubt of that. The body was left sitting upright in the chair, and the witnesses of the tragedy that had been enacted passed out into the stone corridors as miserable, as weak-kneed a lot of men as can be imagined. It had nauseated all but a few of them, and the sick ones had to be looked out for. They were all practically silent for some time. Their minds were too busy to enable them to talk. They all seemed to act as though they felt that they had taken part in a scene that would be told to the world as a public shame, as a legal crime.*

The second surge caused Kemmler's body to emit smoke, and the smell of burning flesh filled the room, according to an account in the *American Bar Association Journal*. He gasped for air. Several witnesses vomited and fainted; others left the room. His clothes caught fire. Kemmler's body was smoking. An electrode bored a hole in his back through to his spine. He died four minutes after the second surge. His body was so hot to the touch that guards could not remove it from the chair for several hours until it cooled. One of the electricians who set up the chair sent a telegram immediately after the execution, writing, "Execution was awful botch. Kemmler literally roasted to death," according to the *New York Times*, which added that "probably no convicted murderer of modern times has been made to suffer as much as Kemmler suffered. The execution cannot merely be characterized as unsuccessful. It was so terrible that words fail to convey the idea." Newspapers began referring to death by electrocution as being "Westinghoused," according to Richard Moran's *Executioner's Current: Thomas Edison, George Westinghouse and the Invention of the Electric Chair.*

A cartoon of a man being taken to the electric chair. George Westinghouse didn't want his name associated with the electric chair. Nevertheless, being electrocuted was known as being "Westinghoused." *Courtesy of the Archives Service Center, University of Pittsburgh.*

An autopsy conducted by Dr. George Fell claimed Kemmler had died instantly. Fell said the appearance that Kemmler was still breathing after the first surge of electricity was due to muscular contraction and that Kemmler's execution was more humane than hanging. Dr. Carlos MacDonald, who issued the official report on Kemmler's electrocution, wrote that the execution was "a successful experiment" and that the death was "painless," although he admitted that "there were several defects of minor character," reported the *New York Times.* Death, he said, comes "in an infinitesimal fraction of a second." MacDonald reported that after the second surge, Kemmler had no pulse, no heartbeat and that his pupils were dilated. "In other words, Kemmler was dead," said MacDonald in his official report. Fell was unable to conduct the autopsy for three hours after Kemmler had died because parts of his brain and body were still hot.

Kemmler had been a pawn between the opponents of capital punishment and the burgeoning electric industry. Edison told the *New York Times* following the execution, "I have merely glanced over an account of Kemmler's death, and it was not pleasant reading." George Westinghouse was more direct. "They could have done better with an axe." Dr. C.M. Daniels, who witnessed Kemmler's death, later told a reporter "I would rather see ten hangings than one such execution as this. In fact, I never care to witness such a scene again. It was fearful. No humane man could witness it without the keenest agony," reported the *New York Times.* Alfred Southwick witnessed Kemmler's gruesome demise. "This is the culmination of ten years of work and study. We live in a higher civilization today," he said, according to an account held by the Smithsonian.

In another ghastly electrocution in 1893, William Taylor was hit with a surge of electricity that caused one of his legs to contract so vigorously that the movement broke the front leg of the chair, sending Taylor's body pitching forward. The electricity was turned off, but Taylor still was alive. He groaned and regained consciousness. When officials attempted to administer a second shock, the dynamo malfunctioned. Taylor was removed from the chair as physicians eased Taylor's pain with morphine and chloroform. After an hour was spent repairing the device, Taylor was placed back into the chair and electrocuted a second time.

Edison continued making suggestions to prison officials on ways to make the electric chair more humane, but his recommendations were met with little success. When Charles McElvaine was electrocuted in 1892, Edison suggested that McElvaine's hands be placed in buckets of saltwater so the current would travel through his wrists rather than his head, making him die faster. A forty-nine second charge of 1,600 volts failed to kill McElvaine, so officials placed an electrode on his head to kill him.

Despite the horrific instances of several botched executions, the U.S. Supreme Court, in 1915, ruled that the chair was less painful and more humane than hanging. "The shock of a spectator of seeing a man hanged is undoubtedly greater than any he receives from witnessing an execution by modern scientific methods," reported the *New York Times*.

The first person in Pennsylvania to die in the electric chair was John Talap, who killed his wife, Mary Fesco Talap, in 1913. He shot his wife in the back as they walked across a muddy field near Pottstown in Montgomery County. The couple had four children. John Talap accused his wife of being unfaithful and had threatened to kill her previously, according to an account in the *Pottstown Mercury*. Talap told a jury his gun went off accidently as they were walking across a muddy field and he slipped, but he failed to explain how the gun fired three times, with two bullets striking his wife. An autopsy revealed that one of the slugs rested on the tip of her tongue.

Talap was executed two years later. The *Pittsburgh Press* described the state's new electric chair as the "most complete electric chair in the world," costing $50,000. "No money was spared in making the new death house the most complete in the country." Talap was accompanied to the chair by a Greek Catholic priest who watched as Talap's body stiffened with three electrical charges until he was dead. Wisps of blue smoke emanated from his skull.

Charles Douglass was the first person from Westmoreland County to die in the electric chair in 1916. Douglass had been convicted of murder, and while he was housed in the Westmoreland County Jail, he managed to escape after beating a guard unconscious. But he was later captured.

Fayette County sheriff P.A. Johns oversaw twenty-four hangings and said, "Electrocution is very much superior to hanging. It is less revolting and more humane." Allegheny County Jail warden Edward Lewis opposed the death penalty, arguing it did not serve as a deterrent to murder. "A man will do things in a passion, which takes his reason away from him and makes him forget the penalty. Then he has to pay for it with his life. It is not right," he told the *Pittsburgh Post* after Pennsylvania began using the electric chair.

Westmoreland County began executing prisoners condemned for murder in public following the Revolutionary War. The first legally sanctioned hanging occurred on December 20, 1785, when two men were hanged in Hanna's Town in Westmoreland County. Mamachtaga, a member of the Delaware tribe, was hanged for killing two white men in a drunken rage in colonial Pittsburgh. Mamachtaga surrendered peacefully when a posse came to arrest him. The nearest court was located in Westmoreland County, so Mamachtaga was taken there for trial. The village had a jail and tavern, which served as the courthouse, and several log cabins. "Mamachtaga made no attempt to escape," wrote Hugh Henry Brackenridge, a lawyer who wrote an account of the trial and execution. "He was now sober and gave himself up to the guard that came over, affecting not to know what happened."

Brackenridge published a newspaper and founded the Pittsburgh Academy, which later became the University of Pittsburgh. Brackenridge's account of the trial was published in *The Trial of Mamachtaga, A Delaware Indian, the First Person Convicted of Murder West of the Allegheny Mountains and Hanged for His Crime in the Year 1794*. The trial was quick. The jurors never left the courtroom to deliberate before finding Mamachtaga guilty. Judges Thomas McKean and George Bryan sentenced him to be "hung by the neck until dead," according to Brackenridge's account.

Brackenridge learned "that Mamachtaga was a bad man and was thought so by his nation; that he had been a great warrior but was mischievous with liquor; having killed two of his own people, that it would not be much regretted in the nation to her of his death; and that, except for his brothers, no one would give anything to get him off."

While Mamachtaga waited for death, the child of the jailer became ill, and Mamachtaga promised he would go into the woods to find the herbs that would cure the child. He returned as promised, and the child recovered. Mamachtaga was freed a second time to go back into the woods and paint his face in preparation for his death like a warrior. He returned. Hanging him wasn't easy. Sheriff John Klingensmith had to carry out the execution twice, because the rope broke on the first attempt, according to historical accounts. Mamachtaga was dazed and wobbly as he stood up and thought he was in heaven. He was surprised when his executioner placed another rope around his neck. Before Mamachtaga died, another man was hanged after being convicted of bestiality. A third man had been found guilty of manslaughter, and he was sentenced to have his hand burned with a red-hot poker.

Executions were a combination of solemnity and festivity at the time, as thousands of people showed up to watch a person die. Crowds were rowdy and difficult to control. On his way to the gallows, Joseph Evans, twenty-one, marched behind the cart that carried his coffin to a hillside gallows erected in a grove of oak trees located a short distance from the county courthouse in Greensburg. A contingent of soldiers from the Westmoreland Artillery and Greensburg Blues, along with the county sheriff and four ministers, accompanied Evans, who was executed for the murder of John Cissler before a crowd of between eight thousand and ten thousand people. "The day was very fine and the concourse of people very great, perhaps the greatest ever witnessed in this county," reported the *Pittsburgh Weekly Gazette.*

Hangings were performance rituals in which the prisoner was expected to take part. The procedure began with the condemned being taken from the jail to a church, where a minister delivered a death sermon that the prisoner was forced to listen to. Following the service, the individual was marched to the gallows, where there were more prayers, speeches and hymns. Authorities expected the condemned to confess to their crimes and admit to the awful life that led them to the gallows, warning spectators against sins and crimes they had committed and confessing to the justice of the death sentence.

David Jewell acted the part when he was hanged in Pittsburgh in 1854 in the courtyard of the Allegheny County Jail. He told a small crowd that had gathered to watch his execution to avoid bad company, bad habits and liquor. Jewell "bore himself heroically—not a visible weakness," wrote the *Pittsburg Gazette.* "He hoped his young friends would take example by his untimely fate and avoid bad company and bad habits. If he had done so, he would be as safe as the rest of them. Always to shun the curse of all curses, drink, to touch not, taste not, handle not," reported the *Pittsburg Gazette.*

In 1875, Samuel Beighley was hanged at the county jail, but before he died, he was forced to sit on a chair on top of the scaffold and listen to a minister read his confession aloud before a black hood was placed over his head and the trap was sprung, according to the *Pittsburgh Commercial.* John Good and William Freeman were hanged on the same day at the jail in 1895. Both were convicted of murder. Good's body dangled for nine minutes before he was declared dead, according to the *Semi-Weekly Post* in Pittsburgh. John Sadler was executed in 1901 within two minutes of leaving his cell.

Charles Kruger was executed in 1904 for killing a constable, but his story made major headlines after he confessed to another murder before he was executed. After his sentencing, a defiant Kruger turned to the judge as he was being led from the courtroom and said, "I hope to meet you in hell," according to an account in the *Pittsburgh Post.* Just before Kruger was to be hanged in January 1904, Governor Samuel Pennypacker issued a stay of execution until February 11. Kruger was upset by the delay because he had prepared himself to die. "I'm just ready to die. I bid my mother and sister a last goodbye. Now, it all must be gone through again. I was ready to die."

Pennypacker issued the stay due to questions of Kruger's sanity and whether he would reveal the names of his accomplices in the murder of a Lawrence County official in New Castle, Pennsylvania. Kruger admitted to murdering New Castle treasurer Joseph Blevins, but police suspected he had accomplices. The stay was eventually vacated, and once again, Kruger faced the hangman. But before the trapdoor opened, Kruger delivered a three-minute speech on the gallows, blaming drinking for his criminal behavior and telling the crowd that he had made peace with God. His last words were "God save me," according to the *Pittsburgh Post*. Westmoreland County sheriff John H. Treascher described Kruger as, "without a doubt, the most degraded type of man with whom I've ever had to deal. He was a born degenerate and illiterate, yet shrewd," wrote Treascher in an article for the *Pittsburgh Press.*

Jacob Prinki killed a railroad employee who kicked him off a train after he refused to pay for a ticket. He refused to repent and "went to the gallows as he had lived, an infidel," according to the *Pittsburgh Post*. Edward Floyd was hanged in 1905 for killing a man during a holdup as a crowd of two hundred came to the jail and watched him dangle from the rope.

Dominick Petrilli killed his son-in-law, Ferdinando Salvatore, as the man slept next to his wife and child. The two men had been at odds, so Petrilli placed a ladder against the wall of the house where Salvatore lived and fired a shotgun blast through a rear window at the sleeping man, according to the *Greensburg Morning Review.* Petrilli fled after the shooting, hoping to flee to Italy, but he was arrested by the state police aboard a train in Altoona. After he was returned to Greensburg, a mob surrounded the courthouse, yelling in Italian, "*Alla forcha*!" which translates to, "To the gallows!" according to the *Greensburg Daily Tribune*. To get Petrilli safely out

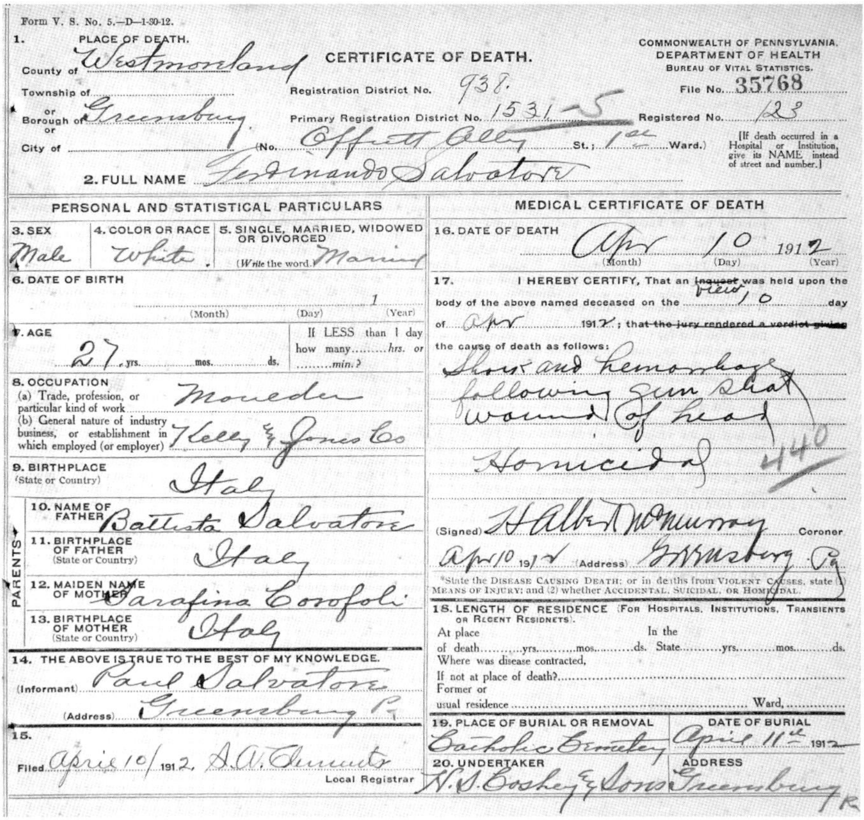

Form V. S. No. 5.—D—1-30-12.

1. PLACE OF DEATH. CERTIFICATE OF DEATH. COMMONWEALTH OF PENNSYLVANIA. DEPARTMENT OF HEALTH. BUREAU OF VITAL STATISTICS.

County of Westmoreland

Township of ...... Registration District No. 938. File No. 35768

or Borough of Greensburg. Primary Registration District No. 1531-5. Registered No. 123

or City of ...... (No. Offutt Alley St.; 1st Ward.) [If death occurred in a Hospital or Institution, give its NAME instead of street and number.]

2. FULL NAME Ferdinando Salvatore

PERSONAL AND STATISTICAL PARTICULARS

3. SEX Male. 4. COLOR OR RACE White. 5. SINGLE, MARRIED, WIDOWED OR DIVORCED (Write the word.) Married

6. DATE OF BIRTH ...... (Month) (Day) (Year)

7. AGE 27 yrs. ... mos. ... ds. If LESS than 1 day how many ... hrs. or ... min.?

8. OCCUPATION (a) Trade, profession, or particular kind of work Moulder (b) General nature of industry business, or establishment in which employed (or employer) Kelly & Jones Co

9. BIRTHPLACE (State or Country) Italy

PARENTS

10. NAME OF FATHER Battista Salvatore

11. BIRTHPLACE OF FATHER (State or Country) Italy

12. MAIDEN NAME OF MOTHER Sarafina Corofoli

13. BIRTHPLACE OF MOTHER (State or Country) Italy

14. THE ABOVE IS TRUE TO THE BEST OF MY KNOWLEDGE. (Informant) Paul Salvatore (Address) Greensburg Pa

15. Filed April 10/1912. S.A. Thumets Local Registrar

MEDICAL CERTIFICATE OF DEATH

16. DATE OF DEATH Apr 10 1912 (Month) (Day) (Year)

17. I HEREBY CERTIFY, That an ~~inquest~~ view was held upon the body of the above named deceased on the 10 day of Apr 1912; ~~that the jury rendered a verdict giving~~ the cause of death as follows: Shock and hemorrhage following gun shot wound of head Homicidal 440

(Signed) H Albert McMurray Coroner

Apr 10 1912 (Address) Greensburg Pa

*State the DISEASE CAUSING DEATH; or in deaths from VIOLENT CAUSES, state (1) MEANS OF INJURY; and (2) whether ACCIDENTAL, SUICIDAL, OR HOMICIDAL.

18. LENGTH OF RESIDENCE (FOR HOSPITALS, INSTITUTIONS, TRANSIENTS OR RECENT RESIDENTS). At place of death ... yrs. ... mos. ... ds. In the State ... yrs. ... mos. ... ds. Where was disease contracted, If not at place of death? ... Former or usual residence ... Ward, ...

19. PLACE OF BURIAL OR REMOVAL Catholic Cemetery DATE OF BURIAL April 11th 1912

20. UNDERTAKER H.S. Coshey & Sons ADDRESS Greensburg Pa

The death certificate of Ferdinando Salvatore, who was murdered by Dominick Petrilli. *Courtesy of Jessica Kiefer.*

of the courthouse, troopers had his brother-in-law pose as Petrilli. While the mob chased the brother-in-law, troopers ushered Petrilli from the state police barracks to the county jail.

Petrilli waited calmly as the date of his execution approached, even as he heard the carpenters erecting the gallows in the jail's courtyard. He was allowed to shake the hand of every inmate at the jail, according to the *Greensburg Morning Review*, before being led to the scaffold. Petrilli remained calm until the last minute, when he collapsed and was so overwrought with the prospect of dying that he had to be carried to the gallows by three guards while a fourth placed the noose around his neck and black hood over his head. The drop failed to break his neck, so Petrilli dangled at the end of the rope for nine minutes before being declared dead of strangulation, according to his death certificate.

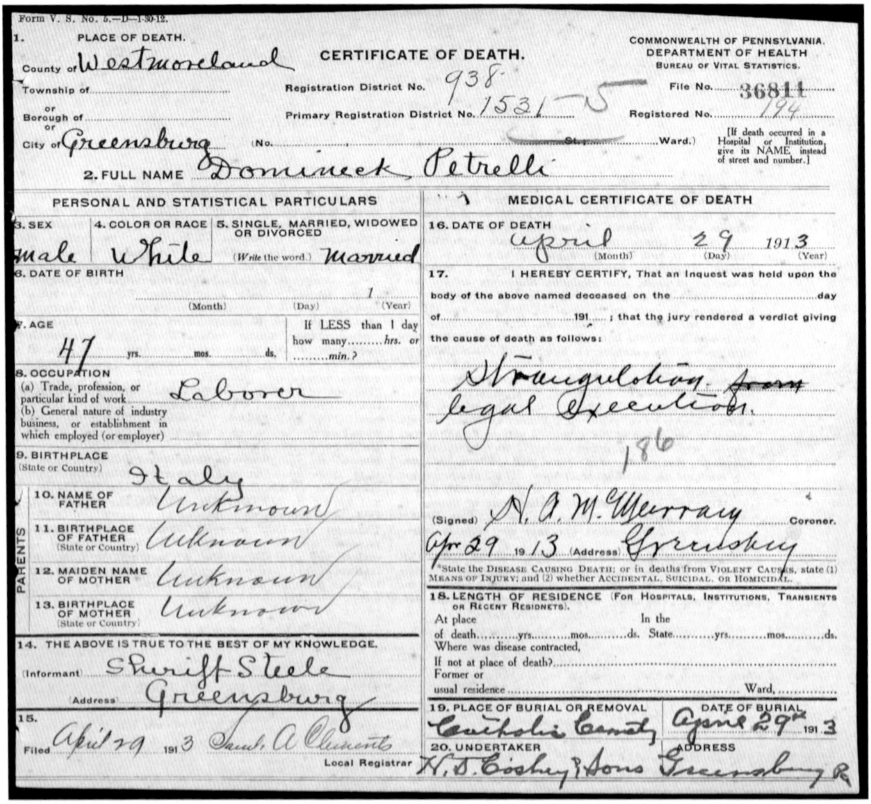

Form V. S. No. 5.—D—1-30-12.

1\. PLACE OF DEATH. — CERTIFICATE OF DEATH. — COMMONWEALTH OF PENNSYLVANIA. DEPARTMENT OF HEALTH. BUREAU OF VITAL STATISTICS.

County of Westmoreland
Township of .... or Borough of .... or City of Greensburg (No. .... St.; .... Ward.) [If death occurred in a Hospital or Institution, give its NAME instead of street and number.]
Registration District No. 938
Primary Registration District No. 1531 5
File No. 36811
Registered No. 194

2\. FULL NAME Dominick Petrelli

PERSONAL AND STATISTICAL PARTICULARS

3\. SEX: Male
4\. COLOR OR RACE: White
5\. SINGLE, MARRIED, WIDOWED OR DIVORCED (Write the word.): Married
6\. DATE OF BIRTH: .... (Month) .... (Day) .... (Year)
7\. AGE: 47 yrs. .... mos. .... ds. If LESS than 1 day how many .... hrs. or .... min.?
8\. OCCUPATION (a) Trade, profession, or particular kind of work: Laborer
(b) General nature of industry business, or establishment in which employed (or employer)
9\. BIRTHPLACE (State or Country): Italy
PARENTS
10\. NAME OF FATHER: Unknown
11\. BIRTHPLACE OF FATHER (State or Country): Unknown
12\. MAIDEN NAME OF MOTHER: Unknown
13\. BIRTHPLACE OF MOTHER (State or Country): Unknown
14\. THE ABOVE IS TRUE TO THE BEST OF MY KNOWLEDGE.
(Informant) Sheriff Steele
(Address) Greensburg
15\. Filed April 29 1913 Saml. A. Clements, Local Registrar

MEDICAL CERTIFICATE OF DEATH

16\. DATE OF DEATH: April (Month) 29 (Day) 1913 (Year)
17\. I HEREBY CERTIFY, That an Inquest was held upon the body of the above named deceased on the .... day of .... 191.... ; that the jury rendered a verdict giving the cause of death as follows:
Strangulation ~~from~~ legal Execution.
186
(Signed) H. A. McMurray, Coroner.
Apr 29 1913 (Address) Greensburg
*State the DISEASE CAUSING DEATH; or in deaths from VIOLENT CAUSES, state (1) MEANS OF INJURY; and (2) whether ACCIDENTAL, SUICIDAL, OR HOMICIDAL.
18\. LENGTH OF RESIDENCE (FOR HOSPITALS, INSTITUTIONS, TRANSIENTS OR RECENT RESIDENTS). At place of death .... yrs. .... mos. .... ds. In the State .... yrs. .... mos. .... ds. Where was disease contracted, If not at place of death? .... Former or usual residence .... Ward, ...
19\. PLACE OF BURIAL OR REMOVAL: Catholic Cemetery — DATE OF BURIAL: April 29th 1913
20\. UNDERTAKER: H. B. Cosley & Sons — ADDRESS: Greensburg Pa

Above: The death certificate for Dominick Petrilli, who was hanged for murder. *Courtesy of Jessica Kiefer.*

Opposite: A newspaper account of Petrilli's execution. *Courtesy of Jessica Kiefer.*

Angelo Gelfi was electrocuted in 1925 for killing his wife after she refused to let him in the house. James Scott was executed that same year for the murder of a police chief. Angelo Cicere died in the chair after killing the president of a social club who threw him out. Dominick Daverse and Joseph Phillips both died on the same night for murder. Daverse of Greensburg, a divorced father of four children, shot and killed his former wife, Theresa, in front of the Westmoreland County Courthouse. He followed his ex-wife as she rode home from work on a bus on a Saturday night in 1947. They got off the bus, and he shot her twice. As she lay on the sidewalk, he shot her another four times before putting the empty gun to his head and pulling the trigger, but the weapon was empty.

GREENSBURG, PA. WEDNESDAY, APRIL 30, 1913.

PETRELLI DROPPED TO HIS DEATH IN EXECUTION CHAMBER OF COUNTY JAIL AT 10:04 TUESDAY MORNING.

Executed for Murder of His Son-in-Law, Ferdinand Salvatore, April 10, 1912—Lost His Nerve at Last Minute and Had to Be Carried to Scaffold by Deputy Sheriffs Copeman and Feightner — Not a Hitch in the Execution—Sheriff Steele Congratulated.

Dominick Petrelli paid with his life for the murder of his son-in-law, Ferdinand Salvatore, in the county jail at 10:04 o'clock yesterday morning.

The condemned man's nerve failed him at the last minute and he was practically carried from cell No. 3 on the west side of the jail to the scaffold by Deputy Sheriffs Charles F. Copeman and Paul L. Feightner. He was brought from the cell at 10:02. Petrelli was accompanied from the cell by Fathers Julian and Germain, O. S. B. Father Julian, who was the condemned man's spiritual adviser, accompanied him to the scaffold, staying with him until the signal was given for the drop.

The noose and black cap were adjusted by Ed. Swartzwood, deputy sheriff of Allegheny county. As soon as the noose was adjusted the signal was given to Sheriff Ben Steele, and Petrelli was dropped to his death at 10:04.

The body shot through the trap and there was never a quiver. At 10:15 Doctors L. C. Thomas, H. A. McMurray, W. H. Brown, C. C. Croushore, W. J Potts and C. A. Wynn pronounced Petrelli dead.

The sheriff's jury comprised of J. C. Frederick, W. H. Johns, John N. Girvin, Braden W. Leasure, Stanley E. Cook, Robert H. Maxwell, E. E. Helman, E. R. Shirey, J. C. Crise, F. J. Maxey, Sam Morgan, Jr., and H. T. Snively, then gave a verdict that the law had been complied with.

Death Due to Strangulation.

A coroner's inquest was then held by Coroner H. A. McMurray in his office in the Court house. The testimony of three doctors was heard by the jury impaneled by the coroner. The verdict was that Petrelli legally came to his death through strangulation.

The following persons were on the coroner's jury: J. C. Frederick, W. H. Johns, John N. Girvin, Braden W. Leasure, Stanley E. Cook and Robert H. Hammond.

Executions in Westmoreland County.

In the years 1774 and 1775, when the county seat was still at Hannastown, an Indian and white man were hanged for murder. The records were destroyed by fire and their names are not known.

Joseph Evans was the first man publicly executed in Greensburg, in the year 1830. Evans was hanged April 20 of that year by John Klingensmith, sheriff.

There were no executions in the county from the time Evans was hanged until January 20, 1875, when Samuel Beighley was hanged by Sheriff John Guffey.

On July 28, 1895, John Good and William Freeman, two negroes, were hanged by Sheriff P. F. McCann.

Two persons were hanged during Ben F. May's term as sheriff. John Sadler, January 10, 1901, and Vassell Nikolaw, September 26, 1901.

Charles Kruger was executed by Sheriff John H. Trescher on February 11, 1904, and Jacob Prinkey, September 29, 1904, by the same sheriff.

Edward Floyd, colored, was hanged by Sheriff George Seaner, April 25, 1905.

Dominick Petrelli was executed by Sheriff Ben Steele, April 29, 1913.

Doctors Who Witnessed the Execution Pronounced Petrelli Dead at 10:15 — Body Taken From the Death Chamber to Catholic Church Where Last Rites for Dead Were Observed — Buried in Catholic Cemetery — But Few Saw the Drop.

The body of Petrelli was lowered from the scaffold to the coffin that had been placed in the cell Monday evening, two minutes after he had been pronounced dead by the physicians. He was then turned over to the Coshey undertaking firm. The body was then taken to the Catholic church where the last rites for the dead were observed. From the church it was taken to the Catholic cemetery.

The only persons who witnessed the execution were those provided by the law. While but few were within the execution chamber a large crowd had gathered around the jail waiting for the word that Petrelli had paid with his life for his crime.

After the body had been removed from the jail the crowd thronged inside to take a look at the instrument that had dealt death to the man who murdered his son-in-law.

The scaffold was then taken down and removed to the tower of the jail. It will again be called into use when Joe Erjaervis is executed, May 8, for the murder of Mat Petek.

Shook Hands With Prisoners.

The execution cast quite a gloom over the county jail. All the prisoners were locked in their cells after they had been given breakfast in the morning. They were kept in until the scaffold had been removed.

In the morning Petrelli shook hands with each prisoner in the county jail for the last time. In that number are several who will be tried for murder at the coming term of criminal court.

Sheriff Congratulated.

Sheriff Ben Steele received many

Continued on Page 4.)

Daverse fled into the Saturday night movie crowd and continued to Uniontown, Pennsylvania, where he shaved his moustache and headed south before landing in Denver, Colorado, where he was arrested eighteen months later. Daverse had a death sentence looming over him for three years and was granted sixteen stays of execution before he was executed in 1953. After he had exhausted his state appeals, his attorneys took the case to federal court and started the appeals process anew.

The main witness against Daverse was his thirteen-year-old daughter. She testified that her father had been planning to kill her mother. "You won't have a mother after Easter. She won't walk the streets of Greensburg for very long," said the girl, according to testimony in the *Pittsburgh Press*, "I told you I'd kill her." When he was arrested in Denver, Colorado, Daverse admitted to detectives that he killed his wife. "Yes, I shot her. We fought and argued all the time. I kept seeing the gun at my sister's house and decided to take it….After I shot her, I put the gun to my head and pulled the trigger a lot of times. It didn't go off. I don't know why. I threw it away."

Irene Schroeder became the first woman to be executed in Pennsylvania in the electric chair in 1931, along with her lover, Glenn Dague, for the murder of Pennsylvania highway patrolman Brady Paul in 1929. Schroder slept so soundly the night before the execution that she had to be roused from a deep sleep, reported the *Pittsburgh Post-Gazette*. She awoke, applied her makeup and calmly walked into the death house and sat directly onto the chair.

The physiological effects of electrocution have been debated by lawmakers and opponents ever since the electric chair was invented. The electrical charge comes from two cables with electrodes at the end of each. One probe is attached to the skull, the other to a leg. The straps around the chest restrain the inmate and lock their chest muscles to prevent the prisoner from breathing. A leather mask is placed over the prisoner's face to spare witnesses the grotesque scene of watching the prisoner's eyeballs pop out and melt. The current raises the body's temperature to 150 degrees, making the organs too hot to touch during the autopsy that follows. The brain's electrical network is fried, baking neurons in the brain.

Experts are also uncertain whether electrocution causes death immediately. French pathologist Dr. L.G.V. Rota wrote in 1928 that death by electrocution "is a form of torture. I do not believe that anyone killed by electrocution dies instantly….The condemned person may be alive and even conscious for several minutes without it being possible for a doctor to say whether the victim is dead or not," according to an article in the *Pittsburgh Post-Gazette*.

Others claim a prisoner loses consciousness immediately, even if their heart continues beating after a surge of electricity; the brain is dead, and the heart beats on its own. They claim the current reaches the brain at the speed of light and that the individual dies before pain signals reach the brain.

U.S. Supreme Court justice William Brennen wrote that all forms of the death penalty violate the Eighth Amendment, which protects citizens against cruel and unusual punishment. He said death by electrocution is "uniquely degrading to human dignity" and likened it to burning at the stake in *Jimmy L. Glass v. Louisiana* in 1985. Brennen included a grisly description of death by electrocution:

> *The hands turn red, then white, and the cords of the neck stand out like steel bands. The prisoner's limbs, fingers, toes, and face are severely contorted. The force of the electrical current is so powerful that the prisoner's eyeballs sometimes pop out and "rest on* [their] *cheeks." The prisoner often defecates, urinates and vomits blood and drool. The body turns bright red as its temperature rises, and the prisoner's "flesh swells and his skin stretches to the point of breaking." Sometimes, the prisoner catches on fire, particularly if* [they] *perspire excessively. Witnesses hear a loud and sustained sound like bacon frying, and the sickly-sweet smell of burning flesh permeates the chamber. This "smell of frying human flesh" in the immediate neighborhood of the chair is sometimes bad enough to nauseate even the press representatives who are present. In the meantime, the prisoner almost literally boils: the temperature in the brain itself approaches the boiling point of water and when the post electrocution autopsy is performed, the liver is so hot that doctors have said that "it cannot be touched by the human hand." The body frequently is badly burned and disfigured.*

George Barbour, a reporter for the *Pittsburgh Courier*, witnessed the execution of Cleveland Thompson, who received fourteen reprieves and went through thirteen court-appointed lawyers before he died. Thompson was convicted of the first-degree murder of a bartender in the Hill District neighborhood of Pittsburgh. As Thompson walked toward the chair, one of his legs buckled, and he fell to the floor. Guards helped him to his feet.

"And there it was! The gaunt, ugly, heavy oaken chair with its hideous-looking metal trappings supported what looked like two-by-fours was the center of attention. Beneath was the glow of brilliant lights," Barbour wrote. As the current surged through Thompson's body, his torso lurched forward. His neck swelled, and his chest expanded. He clenched his fists. Wisps of smoke seeped out from beneath the leather mask that covered most of his face. "An electrocution is a nightmare to watch," Barbour added. He said Thompson was "cooked to death."

As long as there have been proponents of capital punishment, there have been opponents. Dr. Benjamin Rush, a signatory of the Declaration of Independence and a Philadelphia physician, publicly urged abolition of death sentences, writing in 1787 that "an execution in a republic is like a human sacrifice in religion." He questioned whether an execution conducted for religious reasons should be done in the name of God. Elbridge T. Gerry, the vice president of the United States in 1813, said the "mental anguish [of victims] far exceeds the pain [of the executed]."

Pennsylvania attorney general William Bradford wrote that only certain crimes should be punishable by death in his "Enquiry How Far the Punishment of Death Is Necessary in Pennsylvania," which was written in 1793. Bradford did not believe death "is absolutely necessary" in all cases. At the time, a prisoner could be executed in Pennsylvania for stealing a horse, counterfeiting, forging documents, robbery and burglary. "I have already observed that the fear of death is universal and impressive and that its beneficial effects and defeated principally by the hopes of impunity," wrote Bradford.

Bradford recommended that murderers be sentenced to life in prison at hard labor. "The labor, in most cases, should be real hard labor—the food wholesome—should be coarse—the confinement sufficiently long to break down a disposition to vice—and the salutary rigor of perfect solitude invariably inflicted on the greater offender."

The Pennsylvania General Assembly defeated a proposal in 1842 that would have made murder punishable by life in prison and hard labor. Another measure was defeated four years later that would have proscribed life in prison for first-degree murder. It was an effort to allow juries, after convicting a prisoner of murder, to recommend to the governor that a death sentence be commuted to life in prison; it passed the house but met defeat in the senate.

Punishment by death for the crime of murder has been part of the justice system since ancient times. *Lex Talionis* originated in Babylonian law and proscribed "an eye for an eye," which comes from Exodus 21: "And if any mischief follow, then thou shalt give a life for a life, eye for an eye, tooth for tooth, hand for hand, burning for burning, wound for wound, stripe for stripe." The Code of Hammurabi codified death for certain crimes. The Twelve Tablets of Rome proscribed punishment for specific crimes and listed separate categories of punishment for noblemen, freemen and slaves. Draco's Code under the Draconian Constitution in Athens in the seventh century put in writing what had been oral law interpreted by powerful Athenians who could manipulate the law to suit their desires. Draco provided a written set of laws and a constitution that allowed anyone who could read to have access the laws. In Mosaic law, the Torah and Talmud allow for capital punishment for murder, and the Koran allows the death penalty but provides the option of mercy or clemency. The Bible supports the death penalty, and Christian churches have accepted the right of civil authority to enforce capital punishment and does not consider the death penalty murder. The New Testament, however, does not address capital punishment, even though it contains the story of the most famous execution in history: Christ's crucifixion.

13

"THE LAST MILE"

John Wesley Wable's final ride of his life was a 123-mile trip from the Westmoreland County Jail in Greensburg to the state prison at Rockview on Monday, September 26, 1955, where he would die that night in the electric chair. The Centre County Prison is an imposing fortress-like structure situated on four thousand acres in a valley between Mount Nittany and Snowshoe Mountain. It is a six-mile drive from State College, the home of Penn State University. The *Pittsburgh Press*, in 1930, called Rockview a "model prison," because it was surrounded by wide-open spaces and vast woodlands, where trustworthy inmates could work on the prison farm.

Wable left the county jail at 12:40 p.m. on a cool fall day, the temperature only reaching sixty-one degrees Fahrenheit. Westmoreland County sheriff Howard Thomas and Warden William Hohn waited outside the jail, along with state police corporals Jack Bert and Harry Anderson, to escort Wable to the prison. Troopers Carl Metz and Edward Gorga followed in a second car. Wable was calm, and Hohn said the prisoner slept soundly the night before he left.

Wable was a model prisoner, the warden said. He awoke every morning at 5:00 a.m., had breakfast at 7:00 a.m., mingled with the other eighty-five inmates, ate lunch, had dinner at 5:00 p.m. and was asleep by 10:00 p.m. Wable wore a gray suit as he left the jail. He mentioned the weather to his escorts as he stepped outside into the chilly air. He was handcuffed and shackled before troopers guided him to the back seat of a car. "He didn't even say goodbye," Deputy Warden George Kopko said almost sorrowfully. "He didn't say a word," according to the *Pittsburgh Post-Gazette*.

When inmates ares sentenced for capital murder today, they immediately become a prisoner of the state correctional system, where they could wait decades before they are executed—if they are executed at all. Legal appeals can make time stand still as an inmate waits for their appeals to be decided. In Wable's case, the appellate process was quick. After appealing to the Pennsylvania Supreme Court, Scales made no effort to seek relief in the U.S. District Court in Pittsburgh, which could have prolonged Wable's life or resulted in a new trial. A federal appeal would have also prevented the governor from setting a date for the execution.

Currently, it takes an average of twelve years for the courts to review a death sentence, according to a study by the *Justice System Journal*. The initial appeal deals with the legal issues within the context of the trial. But a prisoner can file a petition under the Post-Conviction Relief Act once the state supreme court affirms the sentence by arguing issues outside the trial. For example, the condemned can claim that their defense attorney was ineffective, incompetent or failed to present evidence that could have exonerated them.

In his appeal to the Pennsylvania Supreme Court, Scales again raised the issue that Judge Bauer had erred by allowing the prosecution to introduce evidence from the killing of Lester Woodward and the wounding of John Shepard into evidence. "The court committed no error, therefore, in the admission of the testimony relating to the murder of Woodward and the shooting of Shepard."

After the justices rejected the appeal, Scales appealed to supreme court for a stay, which was rejected. "We are of the unanimous opinion that the petition fails to set forth sufficient cause for action. Therefore, the stay is denied," wrote Justice Allen M. Stearne in *Commonwealth v. Wable.*

A dejected Scales told the *Pittsburgh Press*, "We have now done everything we can for him."

Scales told reporters that he was considering an appeal to the federal court in Pittsburgh. "There is a possibility of a petition to federal court which we haven't determined yet," although he did not seek relief in the U.S. District Court in Pittsburgh. Scales drove to Harrisburg arguing before the Pennsylvania Pardons Board, seeking to have the sentence changed to life in prison, arguing that, eventually, "Jim Parks" would be located, and it would be unfair to execute a man who may not deserve death if somebody else pulled the trigger. "He might be an accessory, but others were involved," Scales argued. James Finnegan, a member of the pardons board, questioned why Wable was unable to produce more evidence to prove that Parks existed if they had been together for six to eight months. "During those six to eight months, why was it that he couldn't find anyone to mentally identify him as a human being?" Westmoreland County district attorney L. Alexander Sculco told the board that Jim Parks was a "figment of Wable's imagination. There is nothing in this case that I can see why the board should give leniency," reported the *Pittsburgh Press.*

Assistant District Attorney Joe Loughran said the brutal nature of Wable's crimes warranted death. "We cannot find one extenuating circumstance that demands giving Wable any type of mercy. Every possible lead has been run down. I ask this board to read the record and find one instance of extenuating circumstances that would enable it to give this man mercy. There is no 'Jim Parks.' We have run down every lead we have and been unable to find him."

Scales then sought a stay from Governor George Leader, who rejected Wable's request. "The attorney was asked why he thought a respite should be given," according to the governor's aide Richard Heagy. "He said he had no new evidence then but hoped something would turn up. The governor denied it because there was nothing on which to base the request," reported the *Sun-Telegraph*.

Wable was prepared for his trip to the death house, a small building located in an area in the rear of Rockview that used to serve as the prison's hospital. Wable tried to fire his attorneys in a last-ditch effort to escape death as his execution date neared, but Judge Bauer denied his request, saying "their duties shall continue until all matters have been disposed of. It is not necessary to issue any further order as to the defendant being represented by counsel."

The vehicle carrying Wable drove north on Route 66 until it reached the intersection of Route 22. Wable talked about the upcoming World Series between the New York Yankees and Brooklyn Dodgers but said little else during the journey. When the group reached Ebensburg in neighboring Cambria County, they stopped to eat at Tibbett's Lunch, where Wable asked for shrimp but was told the item was not on the menu that day. However, a kindly waitress prepared Wable a shrimp dinner along with French fries and coffee.

Wable arrived at Rockview at 4:10 p.m., still optimistic that his life would be spared. "I'll be around a long time. I ain't going to die," he told prison officials upon his arrival, according to the *Pittsburgh Sun-Telegraph*. Wable was placed by guards in a cell located near the death chamber. Convicted killer George Capps, who was also scheduled to die that night, waited in a nearby cell. Journalists tried to tell his story by writing how Wable would walk the "last mile" to his death, but the "last mile" was only thirty-five feet.

In the final days of Wable's life, his lawyers worked feverishly to save him. On September 23, Scales filed a petition accusing the prosecution's witnesses of lying during the trial. "Some of the witnesses who testified against him did not speak the full truth, and your petitioner believes he will be able to prove this as fact," wrote Scales. He cited the testimony of Charles Welch, Wable's former cellmate at the Fayette County Jail in Uniontown who testified that Wable admitted to him that he had committed the turnpike killings. Scales also presented Governor Leader with a petition containing one thousand names of Ohiopyle residents who believed Wable was innocent.

Scales received several tips about where to find Jim Parks, but they were likely from pranksters. He received a telephone call from a man who said he had seen Parks and Wable together. "I have only talked to him by telephone. He told me he saw Wable and Parks together," said Scales according to the *Pittsburgh Press*. Scales said the man never called back. Two days before the scheduled execution, Scales drove to Cleveland after receiving telephone calls from two individuals who claimed that Jim Parks was living in the city. "Either this is a wild goose chase, or we really have something," Scales said. "I won't know until I can find these people," Scales told the *Cleveland Plain Dealer*.

Another caller told Scales, "I think I knew Jim Parks, a relative of mine, who lives in West Elizabeth." Scales said, "The man said he would call again tonight." The individual never called back. West Elizabeth is a tiny borough located along the Monongahela River in Allegheny County. Scales told the court that day that he had received a telephone call from a man claiming to be Jim Parks who said he was calling from Cincinnati, Ohio, and would call back. "I have only talked to him by telephone. The man never called back."

The *Pittsburgh Sun-Telegraph* received an anonymous phone call from a man who identified himself as Sam on the day Wable was executed who claimed to know Jim Parks, but the call came too late to save Wable. Sam told Scales:

> *I remember Jim Parks. He was in Wheeling, West Virginia. He was a truck driver and a carnival worker. He lived in the Salvation Army Home. I knew the name sounded familiar to me, but I couldn't place it. I stayed up all last night trying to remember, and it came to me all at once. The Salvation Army Home in Wheeling. I knew he was there at the time.*

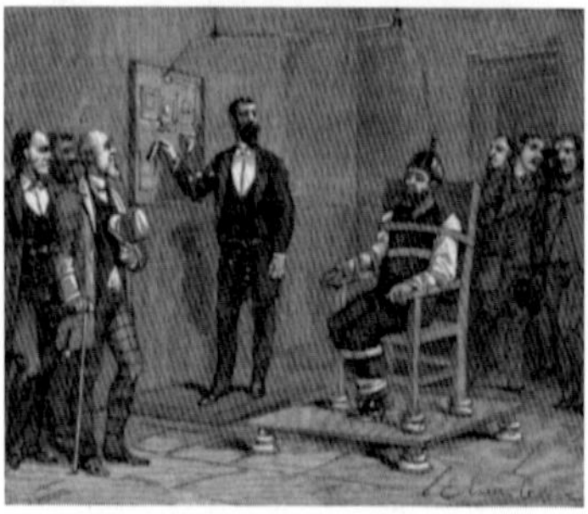

Top: A depiction of a man prepared for execution in the electric chair. *Courtesy of the New York Public Library.*

Bottom: A depiction of a prisoner being strapped into an electric chair. *Courtesy of the Death Penalty Information Center.*

Leon Cassady was a corrections officer at the state prison in Rockview for thirty-three years. He was one of the five guards assigned to walk Wable the thirty-five feet from his cell to the death chamber. Cassady said he felt a "nervous sensation" as he escorted Wable to his death. "It hits you later," Cassady told the *Pottstown Mercury* in 2004. At the last minute, Wable gave Scales what he said was Parks's address. Scales immediately called Governor Leader, but he was on vacation, so Scales talked to Pennsylvania attorney general Herbert Cohen, who refused to consider a stay. After the execution, Cohen telephoned Scales and told him the address Wable provided didn't exist.

Killing a man legally is a challenging task for corrections officials due to the grim nature of the proceeding. Guards witness the final hours of a person's life and record their activities, prepare them for death by shaving their head and leg so electrodes can be attached to their body. They serve them their last meal and listen as clergymen try to comfort the condemned.

Deputy Warden W.J. "Packy" McFarland escorted forty-eight inmates to the electric chair before retiring in 1934 but never watched any of them die. Instead, he manned a telephone connected to the governor's office in case there was a last-minute reprieve. McFarland said he had seen his share of killing during World War I and didn't want to witness any more deaths. He escorted killer Irene Schroeder to the chair, the first woman to be electrocuted, and said she was defiant to the end. "She was composed and reconciled. I never saw her shed a tear."

The cell block on death row is filled with sobs, prayers, hymns and occasional laughter, McFarland told a reporter for the *Pittsburgh Press*. He said most prisoners facing death accept their fate and remain stoic to the end. No one ever asked for a drink or a sedative before sitting in the chair. Jack Yeager was a reporter for the *Centre Daily Times* in State College who

Pennsylvania's electric chair. *Courtesy of the Pennsylvania Department of Corrections.*

witnessed Wable's execution. Yeager attended one hundred executions at Rockview and said every one of the condemned inmates walked calmly to the chair. "I think most of them were resigned to the fact that they were going to die. I never saw anyone who had to be dragged by officials to the electric chair. A minister or priest accompanied most of the individuals, and in one case, I heard a man singing a gospel hymn to the last moment," Yeager told the *Pittsburgh Post-Gazette* in 1974.

Reverend C. Smith Hixon, the pastor of the Meadow Run Methodist Church, spent the day consoling Wable, who ate a last meal of braised ham chunks, boiled potatoes, creamed peas and a cup of cocoa. A last meal is part of a longstanding tradition that may date to Christ's last supper or the Sumerian Code of Laws. The offering of food is the final compassionate gesture shown to a person who is about to die and is meant to add dignity to the process, according to "Last Meals," an article in *Lapham's Quarterly*. Ironically, food, which sustains life, is a symbol to mark the end of life.

George Capps died first that night, executed for the murder of a fifteen-year-old girl. Wable entered the death chamber at 10:04 p.m. He entered the green- and white-painted room wearing a white shirt, black pants and slippers. He glanced around the chamber, staring at the six reporters who were official state witnesses. Wable appeared outwardly calm, according to newspaper accounts. A reporter for the *Pittsburgh Press* recorded his last moments.

"The young farmhand glanced once at the newspapermen seated around the room, his clenched hands and then relaxed, as if he was trying to hide his terror." Prison chaplain the Reverend Kenneth Andrews recited the Twenty-Third Psalm to comfort Wable in his last moments: "Yea, though I walk through the valley of the shadow of death, I will fear no evil: for thou art with me; thy rod and thy staff they comfort me." Hixon later told reporters Wable was "rather exceedingly clam under the circumstances." A.C. Scales had said his goodbyes to Wable earlier in the day. Wable asked Scales to pass a message to his parents: "Tell them I'm okay." To the last, Wable stood by his story that he was only an accessory, according to the *Pittsburgh Sun-Telegraph*.

Gerry Kraemer was the last person Wable saw as he sat in the large oak chair. Kraemer secured Wable's head, arms and legs to the chair with thick leather straps to hold his body from jerking violently when the electric current pulsed through his body. Then Kraemer placed a water-soaked sponge on his head before an electrode was fastened to his skull. A second electrode was attached to his leg as Reverend Andrews prayed, "God is our refuge and our strength."

A prison official stood by a telephone in case the governor granted a last-minute reprieve to halt the execution. Kraemer, an electrician from Pittsburgh, was the state's latest executioner. Kraemer had executed his first man, Oscar McGrew, the year before. Kraemer also had the distinction of executing the last man in the state to die in the electric chair, Elmo Smith, in 1962. Smith was a convicted sex offender who was on parole when he raped and murdered a teenage girl. He was described in various newspapers as a "sexual psychopath with caveman-like tendencies." After the witnesses were ushered into the death chamber and seated, Kraemer flipped a switch. The generator began to whir as ten twelve-volt light bulbs lit up on a board on the chair. "The chair is in working order," Kraemer announced.

Kraemer turned a dial sending two thousand volts into Wable's spindly body. A physician, Dr. J.G. Weixel, placed a stethoscope against Wable's chest and whispered something to Kraemer, who applied another two-thousand-volt surge. Four minutes after sitting in the chair, Wable was dead. Warden Frederick Baldi later told reporters the doctor detected a faint heartbeat and ordered a second application of current. "It is unusual to need two jolts," Baldi said. Wable's body was lifted from the chair and underwent the formality of an autopsy before being turned over to his brother. A hearse from the Humbert Funeral Home in Ohiopyle pulled up to the building, and Wable's body was placed inside.

The control panel for the electric chair at Rockview. The chair was dismantled when Pennsylvania switched to lethal injection as its method of execution. *Courtesy of the Pennsylvania Department of Corrections.*

JOHN W. WABLE DIES IN ELECTRIC CHAIR AS PHANTOM KILLER OF STATE TURNPIKE

Top: A newspaper headline announcing Wable's execution. *From the* Morning Herald *(Uniontown, PA)*.

Bottom: Wable's grave in Ohiopyle. *Courtesy of Find a Grave*.

Ohiopyle residents believed the death penalty for Wable was too severe. "There is a good deal of sympathy toward John around these parts," said R.C. Holt, a grocery store owner. "We would have liked to have seen his sentence commuted to life imprisonment," Holt told the *Uniontown Evening Standard* following the execution.

During fall in Ohiopyle, the woodlands are at their darkest green, and the leaves are flecked with red and yellow. The nights are chilly as mist hovers over the Youghiogheny River in the early morning hours. A quiet descends over the hamlet, broken only by the sound of rushing water hurtling over the boulders embedded in the river. John Wesley Wable came home for the final time. He was buried in the Mount Washington Cemetery in Farmington. A simple headstone marks the gravesite, reading "John W. Wable, 1929–1955."

EPILOGUE

Wable's execution touched off a scramble for the reward, but it would take two years before any of the money was distributed. Anyone who had anything to do with the case filed for a piece of the $6,000 prize. Lawsuits were filed in federal court in Pittsburgh, and U.S. District Judge John L Miller suggested the parties try to reach an agreement on a settlement. "The really important thing is Wable was caught. Isn't it possible for you to agree? Otherwise, this will be a week's trial." said Miller, according to the *Pittsburgh Press*. None of the attorneys wanted to spend a week in court over such a small amount of money, so they reached a deal to divide the money.

John Shepard, the wounded driver, and Joseph Kunkle, the turnpike toll booth operator who placed Wable on the turnpike at the time Harry Pitts was slain, received the largest share, $500 each. Wable's former girlfriend, Leora Crissey, and her stepfather, John Jandura, each got $400 for providing the murder weapon to detectives that Wable had hidden in their home outside of Cleveland.

The remaining individuals each received $345; they included nurse Caroline Smith and her friend, Helen Harmon, who followed Wable after the robbery of the gas station near Belen, New Mexico; brothers Andrew and Hijinio Guttierrez, who followed the car Wable was driving after the holdup; Fred Powell, who pointed out the direction in which Wable fled; P.G. Higdon; J.R. Plants; Sam Scaggs, the pawnshop employee who discovered Shepard's stolen watch; Joseph Bianco, a Harrisburg newspaper reporter who learned about Wable's admission to his cellmate that he was the Phantom Killer; Belen police officer Valentin Torres; and the Cleveland Police Pension Fund, which expended one thousand crucial hours investigating the Cleveland end of the case, linking Wable to the murders.

Caroline Smith said she was unaware that an award had been offered for Wable's capture when she and Harmon trailed Wable after he abandoned his vehicle following the gas station holdup and told police where he was hiding. "I'm not worrying about the reward money very much," she said. "I didn't have it before all of this started, so if I don't get it, I still have done a citizen's duty." Smith said the news about the reward spread through Belen, making everyone suspicious of everyone else trying to cash in on Wable's capture. She received a letter from an elderly man after her name appeared in the *Albuquerque Journal* asking for a portion of the reward money. "I got quite a kick out of the old geezer's letter. He told me money was the root of all evil, yet he wanted me to give him some so he could live," she said.

After the trial, Alexander Sculco and Joseph Loughran had a political falling out when both men decided to run for county judge. Loughran claimed that Sculco had promised to back him the next time there was an opening on the bench. Sculco denied the claim and said Loughran should resign from the district attorney's office or withdraw from the race. Loughran refused to quit, ran against Sculco and lost.

Defense attorney Richard McCormick was elected district attorney and later ascended to the bench. A.C. Scales continued to practice law, and B. Patrick Costello became a prominent Westmoreland County lawyer. Judge Bauer died in 1958; he was sixty-one. Sculco was elected judge in 1957 and died at the age of eighty-seven in 1991. Loughran served as district attorney and died in 1986. Costello died in 2005 at the age of ninety. McCormick became a judge and died in 1996.

Photographs are still not allowed to be taken in courtrooms or in the hallways of the Westmoreland County Courthouse in Greensburg, although there are exceptions for ceremonial events or naturalization ceremonies. The *Greensburg Tribune-Review* tried to get the ban lifted in 1986, but the judges refused.

Governor Tom Wolf issued a moratorium on executions when he took office. Pennsylvania hasn't carried out an execution since 1999, when Gary Heidnik was put to death by lethal injection for killing two women and kidnapping, torturing and raping six others. "I am not crazy," he told a judge

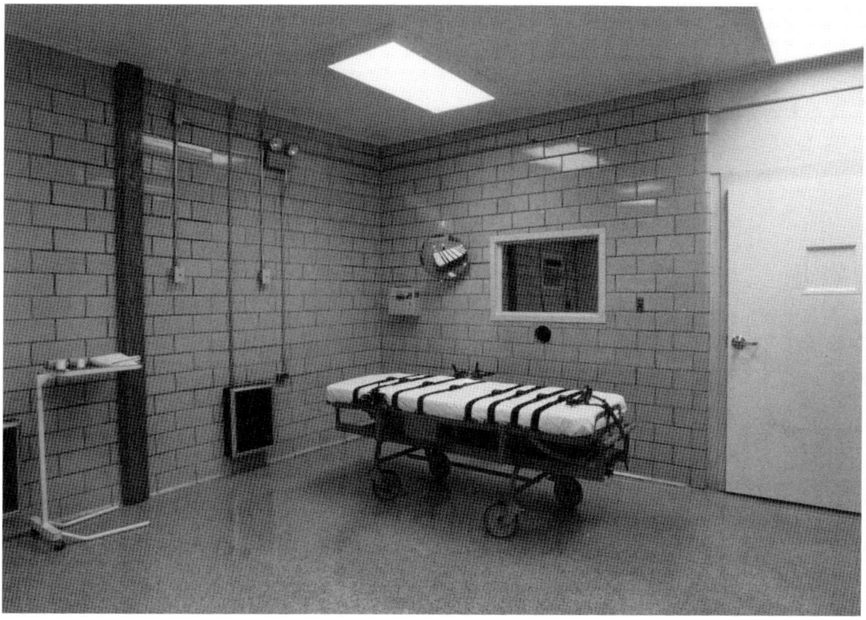

A photograph of the execution chamber, where prisoners are executed with drugs. *Courtesy of the Pennsylvania Department of Corrections.*

when asking to have his appeals dismissed. "I'm not loony. I understand perfectly what's going on with my execution," he said, according to the *Patriot News* in Harrisburg.

Keith Zettlemoyer was the first person executed since 1962, when Elmo Smith died. Zettlemoyer dropped his appeals and died by lethal injection in 1995. "I ask that the people of Pennsylvania and the Commonwealth of Pennsylvania please accept my fourteen years of imprisonment and my execution now as all of my debts to society paid in full," he said, according to the *Morning Call* in Allentown, Pennsylvania. Leon Moser was executed later that year by lethal injection for the murders of his two daughters and ex-wife on Easter Sunday in 1985. "I request the death penalty and that it be carried out as soon as possible," he told the sentencing judge.

Serial killer John Lesko is the longest-serving death row inmate in Pennsylvania. Lesko was sentenced to death, along with codefendant Michael Travaglia, in 1981 but was resentenced in 1995, after his prior sentence was overturned on appeal. Lesko has been under a death sentence for more than forty years for murdering four people over the 1979–80 Christmas holidays. Travaglia died in prison in 2017. "It was obviously, for our county, the most significant criminal episode that had occurred since what they called the

Turnpike Killer," said then–District attorney John Peck in an interview with television station WPXI in Pittsburgh. A reporter asked Lesko during an interview at the time what he thought about being executed. "I have a better chance being hit by a car," he told a reporter for the *Tribune-Review* in Greensburg.

BIBLIOGRAPHY

Newspapers

Albuquerque Journal
Albuquerque Tribune
Brooklyn Daily Eagle
Cleveland Plain Dealer
Greensburg Daily Tribune
Greensburg Morning Review
Greensburg Tribune-Review
Harrisburg Daily Independent
Harrisburg Telegraph
Latrobe Bulletin
Monessen Daily Independent
Morning Call (Allentown, PA)
New York Evening World
New York Times
Patriot News (Harrisburg, PA)
Pennsylvania Packet
Philadelphia Inquirer
Pittsburgh Courier
Pittsburgh Legal Journal
Pittsburgh Post-Gazette
Pittsburgh Press

Pittsburgh Sun-Telegraph
Pittsburgh Weekly Gazette
Pottstown Mercury
Roswell Daily Record (NM)
Semi-Weekly Post (Pittsburgh, PA)
Uniontown Evening Standard
Uniontown Morning Herald
Washington Post

Books

Brackenridge, Hugh Henry. *The Trial of Mamachtaga: Incidents of the Insurrection in the Western Parts of Pennsylvania in the Year 1794*. New Haven, CT: College and University Press Services Inc., 1972.

Cohen, Daniel A. *Blood Will Out: Sensationalism, Horror and Roots of American Crime Literature in Mortal Remains. Death in Early America*. Edited by Nancy Isenberg and Andrew Bernstein. Philadelphia: University of Pennsylvania Press, 2005.

Earle, Alice Morse. *Two Centuries of Costume in America*. Vol. 1. New York: Macmillan Company, 1903.

Hinds, Lynn Boyd. *Broadcasting the Local News: The Early Years of Pittsburgh's KDKA TV*. University Park: Pennsylvania State University Press, 1995.

History of Greensburg and Greensburg Schools. Greensburg, PA: Vogle and Winsheimer, 1899.

Isenberg, Nancy, and Andrew Burstein, eds. *Mortal Remains: Death in Early America*. Philadelphia: University of Pennsylvania Press, 2003.

Mellon, James. *The Judge: Life of Thomas Mellon, Founder of a Fortune*. New Haven, CT: Yale University Press, 2012.

Moran, Richard. *Executioner's Current: Thomas Edison, George Westinghouse and the Invention of the Electric Chair*. New York: Alfred A. Knopf, 2002.

Palmer, Tim. *Youghiogheny River: An Appalachian River.* Pittsburgh, PA: University of Pittsburgh Press, 1984.

Seay, Scott D. *Before Heaven and Earth: Execution, Preaching, and Theology in Early New England*. DeKalb: Northern Illinois University Press, 2009.

Van Urk, J. Blair. *The Story of Rolling Rock*. New York: Charles Scribner and Sons, 1950.

Winchell, Mike. *The Electric War: Edison, Tesla, Westinghouse and the Race to Light the World*. New York: Henry Holt and Company, 2019.

Dissertations

Belczak, Daniel. "The Changing Nature of Punishment: From Gallows to Penitentiaries." PhD diss., Duquesne University, 2011.

Frost, Rebecca. "Identity and Ritual: The American Consumption of True Crime." PhD diss., Michigan Technological University, 2015.

Gottlieb, Gabriele. "Theater of Death: Capital Punishment in Early America, 1750–1800." PhD diss., University of Pittsburgh, 2005.

Hayburn, Timothy. "Who Should Die? The Evolution of Capital Punishment in Pennsylvania, 1681–1794." PhD diss., Lehigh University, 2011.

Journal Articles

Ackerman, Daniel J. "The Trial of John Wesley Wable." *The Sidebar*, no. 3 (June 2011): 14–20.

Bethke, Robert D. "Chapbook Gallows Literature in Nineteenth-Century Pennsylvania." *Pennsylvania Folklife* 20, no. 1 (Fall 1970): 2.

Bosso, Ronald A. "Lecture at the Pillory: The Early American Execution Sermon." *American Quarterly* 20, no. 2 (Summer 1978): 156.

Brown, Harold P. "The New Instrument of Execution." *North American Review* 149, no. 149 (November 1889): 586.

Denno, Deborah. "Is Electrocution an Unconstitutional Method of Execution? The Emergency of Death over the Century." *William and Mary Law Review* 35, no. 2 (1993–94): 551.

"The Fall of Ohiopyle." *Literary Gazette* 6, no. 2 (September 1, 1823): 147.

King, Gilbert. "Edison v. Westinghouse: A Shocking Rivalry." *Smithsonian*, October 11, 2011. smithsominamag.com/history/edison-vs-westinghouse-a-shocking-rivalry-10214630361.

Linders, Annulla. "The Execution Spectacle and State Legitimizing: The Challenging Nature of the American Execution Audience, 1833–1937." *Law & Society Review* 36, no. 3 (2002): 607.

Loftquist, William S. "Justice on the Western Frontier: The Death Penalty in Pre-Industrial Pennsylvania, 1754–1840." *Pennsylvania History: A Journal of Mid-Atlantic Studies* 85, no. 4 (Fall 2018): 556.

Madison, Davis J. "Recognizing the Art of Nonfiction: Literary Excellence in True Crime." *World Literature Today* 86, no. 5 (September–October 2012): 900.

Martschukat, Jurgen. "The Art of Killing by Electricity: The Sublime and the Electric Chair." *Journal of American History* 89, no. 3 (December 2002): 900.

Miner, Curtis. "The Pennsylvania Turnpike from Toll Booth to Tunnels: Rediscovering America's First Superhighway at 75." *Pennsylvania Heritage*, Fall 2015. pa.heritage.wpengine.com.article/pennsylvania-turnpike-tollbooths-tunnels-rediscovery-americas-first-superhighway.

Nugent, Philip R. "Pulling the Plug on the Electric Chair: The Unconstitutionality of Electrocution." *Bill of Rights Journal* 2, no.1 (May 1993): 185.

Pusey, Allen. "Aug. 6, 1890: First Execution by Electric Chair." *ABA Journal*, July 1, 2019. abajournal.com/magazine/article/1890-executed-electric-chair.

Schendel, Gordon. "Something Is Rotten in the State of Pennsylvania." *Colliers Weekly*, November 11, 1950.

Shieh, Pauline. "The Building of the Great Pennsylvania Turnpike, Pennsylvania Center for the Book." Pabook.libraries.psu.edu/literary-cultural-heritage-map-feature-article/building-great-pennsylvania-turnpike.

Government Reports

Elbridge, Gerry, Alfred Southwick and Matthew Hale. "Report of the Commission to Investigate and Report on the Most Humane and Practical Method of Carrying into Effect the Sentence of Death in Capital Cases." State of New York, Troy Press Company, 1888.

Latzer, Barry, and James N.G. Cauthen. "Justice Delayed: Time Consumption in Capital Appeals, A Multistate Study." United States Department of Justice.

"The Pennsylvania Death Penalty Assessment Report." American Bar Association, 2007.

Report of Carlos MacDonald, MD, on the Execution by Electricity of William Kemmler, alias John Hart. September 20, 1890. Annual Report of the Superintendent of State Prisons of the State of New York for the Year 1890.

Youghiogheny River. Letter from the Secretary of War. Report of Survey of the River. 46th Congress, 3rd sess. January 5, 1880.

Legal Cases

Commonwealth v. Daverse. 73 A2nd 405 PA (May 22, 1950).

Commonwealth v. Moon. 386 PA 205 (1956).

Commonwealth v. Wable. Supreme Court of Pennsylvania, 382 PA 80 (1955).

Jimmy L. Glass v. Louisiana. Supreme Court of the United States, 471 U.S. 1,033 (April 29, 1985).

People ex Rel Kemmler v. Durston. 119 NY 569 (1890).

Petition for a Writ of Certiorari in the Supreme Court of the United States. October term 1956, no. 656. In Re: Attachment for Contempt of Court of David Mack, Robert Purdy, Don Bindyke, William Block, James G. Klingensmith, Vince Johnson and Andrew Bernard.

Tribune-Review Publishing Co., P.G. Publishing Co. v. Howard "Bud" Thomas. United States Court of Appeals, Third Circuit 12,393 (May 13, 1958).

Newspaper Articles

Albuquerque Journal. "Wable Ducks Cameras on Arrival in Chicago." October 16, 1953.

Allan, William. "Wable Claims Cops Beat Him." *Pittsburgh Press*, March 11, 1954.

———. "Wable Denied Mistrial in Turnpike Slayings." *Pittsburgh Press*, March 5, 1954.

Basescu, Ron. "Wable Punishment Too Severe." *Uniontown Evening Standard*, September 27, 1955.

Bianco, Joe. "Close Guard Maintained on Wable." *Sunday Patriot News*, November 8, 1953.

Brooklyn Daily Eagle. "Failed to Kill." August 6, 1890.

Brown, Robert. "Nurse Tells Own Story of Wable Tipoff." *Pittsburgh Sun-Telegraph*, October 12, 1953.

Cleveland Plain Dealer. "Lawyer Seeks 2 Men Here Who Might Save Doomed Wable." September 25, 1955.

Delaney, James K. "Wable Confession Read." *Pittsburgh Sun-Telegraph*, March 9, 1954.

Dixon, George. "Wable Likened to Jekyll-Hyde." *Pittsburgh Press*, October 20, 1953.

Gjebre, Wash. "Greensburg Courthouse Photo Ban Is Upheld." *Pittsburgh Post-Gazette*, May 21, 1986.

Johnson, Vince. "Widow of Slain Pike Driver Breaks Down at Wable Trial." *Pittsburgh Post-Gazette*, March 6, 1954.

Kamensky, Bob. "Wable Eludes Big Police Hunt; Named Pike Killer by Cellmate." *Uniontown Morning Herald*, October 10, 1953.

Kennelty, Jack. "Wable Executed by State." *Greensburg Morning Review*, September 27, 1955.

———. "Wable Guilty; to Die." *Greensburg Morning Review*, March 13, 1954.

Matthews, Frank. "Witnesses Urge Barriers for Turnpike." *Pittsburgh Post-Gazette*, March 5, 1953.

Moore, J. James. "Attack Near Lisbon, Hunt Yellow Auto." *Pittsburgh Sun-Telegraph*, July 31, 1953.

New York Evening World. "By Shock." August 6, 1890.

New York Times. "Executioner's Current." December 13, 1888.

———. "Far Worse Than Hanging." August 6, 1890.

———. "The Kemmler Appeal." February 25, 1890.

———. "Kemmler's Death Chamber." April 25, 1890.

———. "Kemmler Told His Fate." March 24, 1890.

———. "Killing by Electricity." October 9, 1890.

Patriot News (Harrisburg, PA). "Reporter Nominated for Pulitzer Prize." January 3, 1954.

Perotta, Sal. "Another Trucker Slain on Turnpike." *Pittsburgh Press*, July 28, 1953.

Pittsburgh Commercial. "A Legal Strangling. The Hanging of Beighley." June 21, 1875.

Pittsburgh Post. "Condemned Man Carried to Gallows by Officers." April 30, 1915.

Pittsburgh Post-Gazette. "AWOL Soldier Confesses Slaying Ohio Official." August 28, 1953.

Pittsburgh Press. "Full Text of Confession Written by Pike Defendant." March 9, 1954.

———. "Gun-Toters Terrorize Drivers." July 29, 1953.

———. "Victim of 'Phantom' Confronts Wable." March 9, 1954.

———. "Wable Plea Denied, He Dies Monday." September 23, 1955.

Pittsburgh Sun-Telegraph. "Blonde, Shot, Chained in Cell After Arizona Desert Battle." January 15, 1930.

———. "Girl Friend Tells of Wable Gun." March 8, 1954.

———. "Mother Glad Police Caught Wable." October 12, 1953.

———. "New Executioner Pulls First Switch." March 15, 1954.

———. "Nurse Refuses to Worry About Pike Reward." October 23, 1953.

———. "Police Find Despondent Couple Shot." August 8, 1953.

———. "Wable Admits Slaying Role." October 16, 1953.

Rosenwald, Michel. "Great God He's Alive." *Washington Post*, April 28, 2017.

Rowe, J. Wyant. "Judge Charges Wable Jury This Morning." *Greensburg Morning Review*, March 13, 1954.

———. "Wable Tells Jury All Witnesses Lied." *Greensburg Morning Review*, March 11, 1954.

Seeger, Murray. "Solon Boy's Memory Looms, As Key in Wable's Pike Trial." *Cleveland Plain Dealer*, March 13, 1954.

———. "Testifies Wable Admitted Killing." *Cleveland Plain Dealer*, March 9, 1954.

———. "Turnpike Slaying Trial Is Monday." *Cleveland Plain Dealer*, February 26, 1954.

———. "Wable to Die for Pike Killing." *Cleveland Plain Dealer*, March 14, 1954.

Snyder, Michael T. "From the Killing Field to the Execution Chamber." *Pottstown Mercury*, May 8, 2004.

Storey, Walter, Jr. "Family of Wable Stands by Him at Murder Trial." *Uniontown Evening Standard*, March 5, 1954.

Sunday Patriot News (Harrisburg, PA). "Phantom Killer Terrorized Pike's Truckers." December 13, 1953.

Thompson, Ben. "Pike Death Suspect Sought in Fayette, Arrest Seen Near." *Sunday Patriot News* (Harrisburg, PA), October 11, 1953.

Treascher, John. "Kruge's Awful Story of Crime." *Pittsburgh Press*, January 11, 1927.

———. "Pike Killer Given Chair." *Pittsburgh Press*, March 14, 1954.

Uniontown Evening Standard. "Defense Charged Prejudicial Stories, Asks for Postponement." March 1, 1954.

———. "Wable Asks New Counsel as Execution Date Nears." September 23, 1955.

———. "Wable Faces Death Tonight." September 26, 1955.

———. "Wable Fate Before Jury." March 13, 1954.

———. "Wable's Temper Flares." March 11, 1954.

ABOUT THE AUTHOR

Richard Gazarik is a former journalist turned author. He lives in western Pennsylvania. This is his sixth book.